GREAT TALES

FROM BRITISH HISTORY

THE BRITONS CHALLENGE ROME

PATRICIA SOUTHERN

AMBERLEY

First published 2015

Amberley Publishing
The Hill, Stroud
Gloucestershire, GL5 4EP

www.amberley-books.com

British Library Cataloguing in Publication Data.
A catalogue record for this book is available from the British Library.

ISBN 978 1 4456 4456 1 (paperback)
ISBN 978 1 4456 4462 2 (ebook)

Typeset in 9.75pt on 12pt Minion Pro.
Typesetting and Origination by Amberley Publishing.

Printed in the UK.

First Contact
55 BC to AD 43

Julius Caesar and His Colleagues

When Gaius Julius Caesar, the Roman governor of Gaul, invaded Britain in the late summer of 55 BC, his colleagues Marcus Licinius Crassus and Gnaeus Pompeius Magnus, more conventionally known as Pompey the Great, were consuls for that year in Rome. During the previous year Caesar had held meetings with Pompey and Crassus, and the three of them had arranged the political world to their mutual satisfaction. Between them they had enough disposable wealth to buy the whole of Rome, so they foresaw no difficulty in persuading the Roman electorate to vote for Pompey and Crassus as consuls, which would give them the opportunity to put into effect their political programme during their term of office. Equally important, they could secure for themselves appointments or commands to be taken up after their consulships, and Caesar could look forward to an extension of the command that he already held in Gaul.

Modern scholars label this alliance between Pompey, Crassus and Caesar the first triumvirate, because of its superficial similarity to the so-called second triumvirate formed by Mark Antony, Octavian and Aemilius Lepidus some months after the assassination of Caesar. The difference between the two alliances was that the first was a purely private agreement, while the second was a legal arrangement officially sanctioned by the Senate, though the senators were more or less coerced at the points of several swords. 'Triumvirate' is an invention of modern historians, with only insecure links to the Latin title *Tresviri* applied to Antony, Octavian and Lepidus, but not to Caesar and co. The Romans of Caesar's day were somewhat less respectful. Recognising the immense power and potential danger of the unofficial alliance, they dubbed it the Three Headed Monster.

Acting on behalf of Caesar, Pompey and Crassus had passed a law to extend his command in Gaul, so he was secure in his appointment until the terminal date of 1 March 50 BC. This date is much discussed by modern scholars, but from Caesar's point of view, the main consideration, in 55 BC, was that he had been granted enough time to plan for rather more grandiose achievements than simply overrunning some of the tribes of his province of Gaul. He would think about the terminal date much later, when it was imminent; these things could always be manipulated.

Pompey the Great already had a glorious track record as a successful general, having rounded up the pirates from the whole of the Mediterranean in far less time than he had been given for the task, and then gone on to take over and win the campaign against Mithradates, king of Pontus, who had been a thorn in Rome's side for several years. After these spectacular successes, Pompey was the foremost military man in Rome, but his political skills in his own city did not match his considerable administrative abilities in organising the territories he had fought over. He was thwarted by the Senate at every turn, because the senators debated at length each and every minor detail of the political arrangements that he had made in the eastern territories, interminably delaying the necessary ratification for them. By the same means he was prevented from settling his veteran soldiers on the land. Frustrated by the Senate, Pompey gained the support of Caesar, who was consul in 59 BC. In one tumultuous year, Caesar had sorted out Pompey's problems and a few more besides, and had obtained for himself the post of governor of Gaul for five years from 58 BC, not just the territory on the Italian side of the Alps, but the whole of Gaul from there to the Atlantic coast.

Marcus Licinius Crassus was a better politician than Pompey but his military reputation was not so glamorous. He had the dubious distinction of having put an end to the rebellion of the slaves under Spartacus. It had been a necessary but not a noble task, since slaves were not considered a worthy enemy, however dangerous they had become, and even there Pompey had claimed the victory because he had been on his way home from his campaigns in Spain when he met the remnants of Spartacus's army, and crushed them. To redress the balance Crassus had formed grandiose plans for true military glory. As his consulship ended he proposed to lead an expedition against the Parthians, Rome's most formidable enemy in the east.

By 55 BC, Caesar was definitely a force to be reckoned with in Roman politics, but he had not yet equalled Pompey in achievements and prestige. Since his appointment as governor of Gaul in 58 BC he had subdued some tribes and made diplomatic agreements with others, but he was nowhere near the completion of his task, and would in fact need another seven years to conquer, subdue and begin to pacify the whole of Gaul. As the summer of 55 BC progressed, it would be only a matter of months before Crassus would set off for the Parthian campaign, and if he was successful against such a vast and organised Empire his stock would rise to unprecedented heights in Rome, eclipsing the fame of the current proconsular governor of Gaul. If Caesar could achieve something spectacular, not hitherto attempted by any Roman general, it would enhance his reputation and keep him in the Roman political limelight. The Romans soon forgot their heroes unless they were constantly reminded of them. The expedition to Britain, remote, mysterious, even romantic, would be something that they had never seen before.

Britain Before Caesar

Britain and the European continent were not entirely unknown to each other in the first century BC. For at least two centuries before Caesar, the Greeks were aware of the existence of the island, which they called Albion. This name was also applied to Spain, but at some point before Caesar's day, the island acquired its name Bretannia, converted by the Romans into Britannia. The use of a generic name for the country might give the impression that the island was inhabited by people who called themselves Britons, conscious of a common identity, using the same language, and sharing the same culture, religion, and way of life. On the contrary, there was never any such unity or uniformity, even during the Roman period. For one thing, the differences in terrain, landscape and soils, especially between the north and south, precluded any close similarity in agriculture and animal husbandry across the whole country, and successive gradual infiltration of tribes from Gaul into the south-eastern areas of Britain introduced cultural divergences and created shifts in the balance of power. Some tribes from Gaul perhaps came at first for booty, and then later to settle, but they retained their original tribal names, so that there were, for instance, groups of Atrebates in both Britain and Gaul. Caesar himself noted that the small farms in south-eastern Britain were very similar to those in Gaul:

> The inland part of Britain is inhabited by tribes who, according to their traditions, are native to those areas, and the coastal areas are occupied by tribes who came from Belgium [*ex Belgio*] for plunder by invading the land. Almost all these tribes are still called by the names that they had when they went to Britain. After they invaded they stayed and began to farm the land. The population is innumerable. The farm buildings cluster together like those of the Gauls, and there are great numbers of cattle. (Caesar *Gallic War* 4.12)

Archaeologists identify a discernible cultural development among British tribes, attributed to Belgic influence spreading from the south-east. Like many other terms, the use of this one is disputed. Although Caesar was writing about events and people he had seen for himself, it is not certain what he meant to convey by the term 'Belgium'. It is a subtle distinction to make, but it referred to a people rather than a territory, and was probably not interpreted in terms of a country. In any case, it should not be considered as exactly coterminous with the nineteenth-century creation that is now called by the same name.

As in Gaul and Germany, the tribes of Britain did not exist in close harmony with each other. According to the Greek geographer Strabo the Romans obtained slaves from Britain, implying that they probably left it to aggressive tribes to raid other tribes and round up their captives to be shipped out by dealers. Struggles for supremacy resulted in the absorption by powerful tribes of smaller and less powerful tribes, with a corresponding fluctuation of territorial boundaries. In his commentaries, Caesar mentions tribes such as the Cenimagni,

Segontiaci and Cassi, who disappear from the record after the first century BC, perhaps because they had been obliterated by their more aggressive neighbours, or had combined with other tribes more peacefully and adopted new names. Tribal names are not necessarily immutable, nor do they always signify common ethnic origins, a factor which can be demonstrated by the case of the Alamanni, who appeared in Germany and Gaul in the third century AD. This tribe was probably an amalgamation of tribesmen of different origins, regardless of race, since the name simply means 'All Men'.

The Iron Age tribes of Britain that Caesar encountered were not yet fully developed, and were certainly not static. British society was in transition, in a process that was still going on when the Emperor Claudius ordered the invasion and occupation almost a century later in AD 43. During the long period that separated the tribal communities of Caesar's day from those of the first century AD, many developments and changes no doubt took place, not all of which can be discerned.

The tribes of Britain in the mid-first century BC are mostly anonymous, and their territorial boundaries cannot be established. There is much more information regarding these topics by the time of the Roman conquest of AD 43, when tribes can be named and their territories roughly defined, so it is possible to make some tentative generalisations about the possible social and political set up in Caesar's day. In Wales and the south-west, hill forts predominate over other kinds of settlement, but nothing has been discovered up to now that suggests a powerful central base for a tribe or group of tribes. It seems most likely that these tribes were not united under a single ruler, but were divided into smaller groups who probably fought each other from time to time. This is implied by the number of hill forts, indicating that people lived in great insecurity, but it is not certain that all of them would be occupied at the same time, or whether they were permanent settlements or acted as places of refuge in times of warfare. The same could be said of the inhabitants of Cheshire, Shropshire and Staffordshire, where hill forts are known but no central place has been identified. By contrast, in the Pennine areas, known in the first century AD as the territory of the Brigantes, there is an abundance of fortifiable hills, but the hill fort culture did not develop, possibly because the tribes were more primitive than their southern neighbours, or perhaps endemic strife among the tribesmen was non-existent or even successfully controlled. On the other hand there seems to have been no tribal centre in the mid-first century BC where a single Brigantian ruler could exercise power, and though two large settlements are known, one at Almondbury near Huddersfield and another at Stanwick further north, these perhaps date from the period of the Roman invasion and early conquest. Caesar had been informed that the northern tribes differed from the southern ones, and that they lived on milk and meat, which suggests a pastoral rather than an agricultural society.

In his two expeditions, Caesar encountered only the tribes of the south-east, whose names we do not know. Only one ruler is named in Caesar's account, when during the second expedition the Britons agreed to give the overall command to Cassivellaunus, but there is no mention of his tribe or his main settlement area, except that his territory lay north of the Thames, so it is assumed that he was chief of the Catuvellauni. Cassivellaunus was emerging as a powerful ruler with designs on the lands of other tribes, and his descendants seem to have fostered the same ambitions. By the time of the Claudian invasion, the tribes of south Britain had established centralised settlements, known to the Romans as *oppida*, the most important one being at Colchester, with other settlements at Verulamium (St Albans), and Silchester. The inhabitants of these settlements established mints and issued their own coins, based on Greek examples. Such a process implies that there was some form of hierarchical structure with centralised control to co-ordinate this corporate effort. The use of coins probably altered the balance of power, not just because of the obvious display of wealth, but because the land where the precious metals were to be found would become supremely important. If you were not already in control of such land, then it would become necessary to obtain control of it and then defend it in case other tribes developed the same aims. The British coinage of the first century AD can yield information about the rulers of the tribes, since they began to put their names on their coins, but the distribution of coinage does not necessarily imply that the persons named on the coins ruled the territory where they were found. It can only be said that such rulers had obtained precious metals and established mints, which implies centralised control and probably a hierarchical society, with all members of that society answerable to the ruler, whose influence extended beyond his boundaries.

The organisation of trade probably stemmed from the same sort of centralised control, or enhanced the ability of certain chieftains to rise to supremacy and remain there. Trading ventures across the Channel had a long history before Caesar embarked on his ten-year conquest of Gaul. The well-known pre-Roman port of Hengistbury Head in Dorset was not just a convenient landing place but a fully developed fortified trading centre, where cattle were brought for sale and metal workers set up shops, and probably an array of secondary supporting businesses were established to provide equipment, food and accommodation, storage and transport. Goods inwards included many amphorae, most probably containing wine, but they were also used for oil and other goods. Pottery from Brittany was in plentiful supply as well. These are the items which leave definite archaeological traces. For other more perishable items, supporting evidence is derived from literature. Writing at a later time, shortly after the death of Augustus in AD 14, the Greek geographer Strabo lists the goods imported by the Britons as jewellery and fine wares, and the goods outwards as grain, cattle, precious metals, hunting dogs and slaves. This information is most likely anachronistic as regards the trading that went on at Hengistbury Head, which declined as a port probably about the same time as Caesar reached the northern parts of Gaul. One reason for this may have been that Caesar defeated the Veneti, the coastal-dwelling tribe whose ships probably carried the goods into and out of Britain:

> The Veneti have the most extensive control over the sea coast and they possess numerous ships, which they use to sail to Britain, and they excel everyone else as navigators. (Caesar *Gallic War* 3.8)

As the depot at Hengistbury Head declined, trade between the Continent and Britain did not cease, but relocated, and also developed and expanded. There is evidence that traders operated at Poole in Dorset, perhaps on a smaller scale than at Hengistbury, but there were also ports or harbours in the south-east. In his description of Britain at the time of his two invasions, Caesar says that most of the traders from Gaul usually landed in the south-east, where the population was more advanced than the rest of Britain.

> The most civilised of the Britons are the people of Kent [Cantium], a coastal region. Their way of life hardly differs from that of the Gauls. (Caesar *Gallic War* 4.14)

It is not clear how this trade with Britain was organised, whether it operated as simple exchange arrangements between small trading firms, or even individuals, or whether there was some larger corporate enterprise. There may have been a combination of all types of trading ventures. Some of the goods may have been paid for in coinage, others may have been bartered. The distribution of coins is not a reliable guide to trading ventures, since coins can arrive at sites via gift exchange, or via theft, and an accrual of coinage may simply mean that someone such as a tribal chief wished to impress his neighbours without actually using the coins to purchase anything. With that in mind it is still clear that even in Claudius's day in the first century AD, the tribes of the south and south-east of Britain were more highly developed than those further inland.

The First Expedition 55 BC

Most of the information about the tribal organisation of Britain in the first century BC is derived from archaeology, with little or no support from Greek or Latin literature. Conversely, information about Caesar's invasions derives wholly from his own account, amounting to a few paragraphs in his commentaries on the Gallic War, and archaeology scarcely enters the picture. Even if it could be discovered for certain where Caesar's army landed and made camp, such brief visits to the island will have left hardly any traces. Caesar gives no clear information about places in his commentaries, except for his mention of the River Tamesis, or the Thames. His commentaries are written in the third person and mostly in the present tense, and they were designed to be read out loud, or perhaps more accurately they would have been almost 'performed'. His audience would be interested only in his own exploits and those of the army. Names of places in the distant island would not have meant much to them.

It has been suggested that Caesar probably planned to invade Britain in 56 BC, but was forced to wait until the following year. In 57 BC he discovered the close connections between some of the tribes of Britain and Gaul during his second year of office, when the tribal leaders of the Bellovaci had fled to Britain and taken refuge there. Then in 56 BC he discovered that the Britons had sent help to the tribes of Armorica (Brittany) when they broke out in fierce rebellion. If he had planned an expedition to Britain in that same year, any intended invasion was thwarted by the outbreak of hostilities with the Veneti, a tribe dwelling on the coast of Gaul. They were expert seamen, and in the process of fighting them the Romans had to build ships and become expert seamen themselves, finally discovering a way of bringing down the masts of the enemy ships and disabling them. At this juncture, Caesar may have entertained thoughts of invading Britain, but it is perhaps more likely that he would put any plans on hold, until he had come to an arrangement with Pompey and Crassus, and then waiting until they had been elected consuls and had passed a law to extend his command for a number of years. This would legalise his future actions, and also give him the opportunity to mount an expedition to Britain, with ample time to repair the damage if things went wrong.

In 55 BC Caesar was delayed once again, this time by the aggressive activities of the German tribes, who were fighting each other and also threatening the peoples of Gaul on the other side of the Rhine. Such a situation could not be left unresolved while Caesar sailed off to Britain. If they were not checked the Germans could undo everything he had achieved in Gaul. The root of the problem was the constant aggression from the Germanic Suebi, who terrorised their neighbours until they succumbed to Suebic domination, or fled. The tribes who became subservient, paying tribute and doing as they were told, potentially swelled the Suebic coffers or the numbers of the Suebic warriors. The tribes who moved away caused further disruption as they sought lands on which to settle. Caesar found a justifiable excuse to intervene when the Ubii of the right bank of the Rhine appealed for Roman assistance as the Suebi approached their territory. He set off in early spring, intending to cross the Rhine, a daring plan that would doubtless be reported in Rome with great aplomb. The Ubii offered to supply boats to ferry the Roman soldiers across the river, but Caesar considered this too dangerous and slow, and more importantly it would not be sufficiently dignified for the Roman army. Caesar needed to make an indelible impression. Instead of using boats he built a bridge, which he describes in some detail in his account of the Gallic War, in a passage which tantalises archaeologists and engineers who have tried with only partial success to reconstruct the bridge on paper via diagrams, or in reality across a river. The Roman army could muster enormous manpower, so it took them only ten days to complete the structure, cutting the first timbers, bringing them to the chosen site and then constructing the bridge. Caesar crossed the Rhine and spent eighteen days in Germany, burning villages and destroying crops to undermine the ability of the Suebi to make war. The tribes melted away, overawed by the speed and ruthlessness of the expedition. When the troops had been withdrawn, Caesar destroyed the bridge, leaving no ready-made access for the Germans to cross into Gaul. Even without the laconic hyperbole of Caesar's commentaries, it still remains an impressive demonstration of strength.

The British expedition can be regarded in the same light, as a similar demonstration of strength, as well as a reconnaissance exercise. Caesar knew that he had left it too late to embark on an invasion of the island, but characteristically he was determined to risk it. The summer was well advanced, so there would hardly be enough time for decisive campaigning, much less occupation of the island, but Caesar thought it would be sufficient achievement to make a landing, and study the inhabitants, the terrain, and the coast, finding where the best landing places were.

There has been considerable speculation about Caesar's motives and what he wanted to achieve in his two expeditions to Britain. Technically the island was outside his province, and according to the law a governor was not allowed to cross his provincial boundaries. He had already done so by crossing the Rhine, and now he proposed to cross the Channel. In both cases he could argue that the tribes of these two areas outside his province threatened its security. His official reason for the British expedition was that British tribesmen had been sent to help the Gauls.

[In preparing for war] the Veneti brought help from Britain, which lies opposite their territory. (Caesar *Gallic War* 3.9)

Caesar was intent upon setting off for Britain. He knew that in nearly all the campaigns in Gaul, help had come for the enemy from there. (Caesar *Gallic War* 4.20)

These observations converted his dash to Britain in 55 BC, and his longer expedition in the following year, from somewhat dubious adventures into justifiable actions. The Romans insisted that they never waged war without just cause, or so they always maintained. Modern scholars suggest that the mineral and agricultural wealth of Britain would be very attractive. Sources of grain were always important, and according to Strabo grain was one of the main exports from Britain. It certainly seems that the Romans hoped to find precious metals. In one of his letters, Cicero lamented the fact that there was no silver in Britain, an assumption that turned out to be untrue, and within a very short time after the Claudian conquest the Romans were mining for it. Cicero also said that there was hardly anything except slaves to be gained from Britain, and he sneered that such slaves would hardly be versed in literature and the arts. The biographer Suetonius offers a less tenable reason for Caesar's invasion, which he attributes to Caesar's inordinate love of pearls, which were to be found in quantity in Britain. The British expedition may have been profitable in this respect, since Caesar decorated his famous statue of Venus Genetrix in Rome with pearls. But a more compelling reason for invading Britain, as suggested above, was glorification of Gaius Julius Caesar, to enhance his reputation and ensure a successful political and military career in the future.

Before he embarked for Britain, Caesar tried to discover pertinent facts about the island. Although the Romans called it an island, which they thought was shaped like a triangle, they knew very little about the northern areas, and were not entirely sure that it really was an island until the Roman fleet sailed all the way round it after Agricola's campaigns, about AD 83 or 84.

The shape of the island is triangular, with one side lying opposite Gaul. On this side one angle in Kent [Cantium] faces east and the other faces south. This side stretches about 500 miles. The second side inclines towards Spain and the west, where Ireland [Hibernia] lies, about half the size of Britain, the sea passage being about the same as that from Britain to Gaul. In mid-channel here, there is an island called Man [Mona]. Several smaller islands are said to lie near the mainland, concerning which some writers have said that the night lasts for thirty days in midwinter. We could find out nothing about this from inquiries, but by measurements made with a water clock we observed that the nights were shorter than on the Continent. The length of this side, the natives believe is seven hundred miles. The third side bears northwards and has no land confronting it, though the angle of this side faces towards Germany, and is supposed to be eight hundred miles long. (Caesar *Gallic War* 5.14)

Livy and Fabius Rusticus compare the shape of Britain to an elongated shoulder blade, or an axe head ... [When Agricola was governor] it was then for the first time that a Roman fleet sailed all the way round the coast and verified that Britain was an island. (Tacitus *Agricola* 10)

As Caesar says in his commentaries on the Gallic War, no one went to Britain without good reason, so nobody knew much about the country:

No one except traders travel [to Britain] without good cause, and even traders know only the south coast and the areas adjacent to Gaul. Even though Caesar summoned traders from all parts of Gaul to his headquarters, he could not discover the size of the island, the number and strength of the peoples who lived there, their methods of warfare, or the landing places suitable for large ships. (Caesar *Gallic War* 4.20)

The traders probably genuinely knew nothing more than was necessary to enable them to navigate to their destinations, land there, unload goods, pick up outgoing cargo, and sail back to Gaul. If they did know more, it is quite possible that they were reluctant to give Caesar all the information that he needed. A summons to Roman headquarters may not have been a comfortable experience, and the loyalties of many traders may have lain elsewhere than with the Roman governor, who had only recently arrived and was currently blazing through Gaul as a conqueror, upsetting more than just trade. After being interviewed by Caesar, several traders went off to Britain and informed the tribes of the forthcoming Roman invasion.

In admitting that he did not learn much about the size of the island, the number and nature of the tribes, their strengths and weaknesses, or their military organisation and how they fought, Caesar emphasised the difficulty of his planned invasion, which in turn made his successes all the greater. He sent off two men to try to find out more. One was Commius, a Gallic tribal chief who had been installed with Roman backing as leader of the Atrebates in Gaul. A branch of the Atrebates were also settled in Britain, so the choice of Commius to act as ambassador to the British tribes might seem a good one, except that the British Atrebates were not settled close to the tribes that Commius was instructed to visit, and loyalties between tribes were far from reliable in negotiations. Why should proud tribesmen of southern Britain listen to a Roman-backed chief of the Gallic Atrebates, and agree to accept Caesar as overlord without a struggle? The unofficial embassy was not a success, and Commius was held captive, only released when Caesar had fought a few battles on British soil.

While Commius endeavoured to win over the Britons, a Roman officer, Gaius Volusenus, who had done good service against the Veneti, was sent off in a warship to spy out the land and discover the best landing places. He was away for five days on this task, but did not risk making a landing, because he would hardly be a welcome visitor, coming from a Roman war galley. He does not appear to have discovered Richborough, where some of the Romans of Claudius's army landed, nor did he find the Wantsum channel which at that time separated the north-eastern tip of Kent from the mainland. The modern so-called Isle of Thanet really was an island then.

Meanwhile Caesar assembled his troops in the territory of the Morini, at a place called Portus Itius, not certainly identified, but generally accepted as Boulogne, which was renamed some time later as Gesoriacum. Having heard from traders that a Roman invasion was planned, representatives from some British tribes came to him in Gaul to submit to him and offer hostages. Caesar accepted their submission:

[Caesar's] intentions had been reported to the Britons by traders, and
delegates came from several tribes, promising to give hostages and to
accept the empire of the Roman people. He listened to them, made
generous promises, encouraged them to keep their word and sent
them back home. (Caesar *Gallic War* 4.21)

The Romans had built some ships for the invasion, and acquired several
more from the Veneti. In total Caesar says that he had eighty ships to
transport two legions, and eighteen more to transport the cavalry, who
were to assemble at a place which he does not name but describes as
'the further port' which may have been Ambleteuse. Arrangements
were made to keep order in the areas of Gaul which he had recently
subdued, and to protect the main port for the return of the fleet. At the
first sign of fair weather, Caesar embarked his two legions, travelling
without baggage or vast food supplies. The cavalry was to follow, but
their transports were blown off course, some of the ships spending a
horrendous night on a stormy sea, and then sailing back to port.

The point where Caesar's fleet approached Britain is not named,
but he described it as a place with cliffs, where the British tribes were
drawn up on the heights, and able to hurl missiles down onto the
Roman ships. Caesar ordered the fleet to sail on for another seven
miles until a more hospitable, flatter part of the coast offered better
landing facilities, perhaps in the area between Deal and Sandwich,
but this is only informed speculation. Caesar summoned the officers
to a meeting to explain that when they were ordered to disembark,
they should do everything very rapidly because of the danger of the
shifting seas, where they would have to fight in the water in order to
gain a foothold on shore. The Britons followed the progress of the
fleet along the coast, and were ready for the Romans when the ships
came to shore. Since the ships were too big to beach them properly,
the soldiers had to jump into deep water and struggle to remain
upright while the Britons on shore had the advantage and could
hurl weapons at them. There was great disorder, so much so that the
soldiers could only form up around whatever standard they could
see, not necessarily their own. While they fought, Caesar ordered
the crews of some of his oared ships to row up towards the beach
to threaten the flank of the British tribesmen, and then the famous
standard bearer of the Tenth legion, who is unfortunately not named

for posterity, jumped down and started forward, encouraging the troops to follow him. By degrees the Romans managed to gain a foothold on the beach, and the Britons withdrew. There could be no pursuit because the cavalry had not arrived, so Caesar made camp, at an unknown site.

Delegations from some of the British tribes approached Caesar making overtures for peace, with offers to give hostages. Commius was returned intact to the Romans. Some of the tribes settled down near the camp, so it seemed as though the uneasy peace might be an enduring one. But Caesar had noted that among the warriors who had opposed him on the beaches, there were some from the tribes which had supposedly submitted to him while he was still in Gaul:

> Caesar complained that although [the tribesmen] had voluntarily sent delegates to the Continent [Gaul] to arrange a peace, they had now begun to make war on him without cause; but he said he would forgive them for their ignorance, and demanded hostages. (Caesar *Gallic War* 4.27)

It was certain that at the first sign of Roman weakness, the peace overtures would be withdrawn. The tenuous hold of the Romans was exposed quite unexpectedly. It was the time of the full moon, and its effect on the tides was not properly understood. Since the ships could not be beached out of reach of the waves, some of them were wrecked in the high tides. Caesar describes the event quite candidly, but then he could hardly have glossed over the disaster when it had been witnessed by two legions, and in describing adversity and then how it was surmounted, he could only enhance his reputation. He sent to Gaul for replacement tackle, tools and equipment, and cannibalised the ships to create seaworthy ones, losing about twelve in total.

The Britons observed all this without actively making too much of it, but in small numbers they started to melt away from the camp. They left several of their men quietly working in the fields to avoid suspicion, while they covertly collected an army and planned how to defeat the Romans. It is not known who led them at this time, but the way in which they calmly and stealthily withdrew and then reassembled suggests that one chieftain had the authority to adopt a plan and keep the warriors in check.

The Romans had not brought food supplies with them, so foraging parties had to be sent out to gather crops. In a part of the field where the foragers habitually worked, the crops had been left standing, alerting the Britons to the exact area where the legionaries would aim for next, so the tribesmen waited, hidden in woods, while a group of soldiers from the Seventh legion set out to bring in the grain. These were ambushed, and might have been annihilated if the men in the outposts that Caesar had established had been less vigilant. The fighting had stirred up large dust clouds, alerting the men of these outposts and then Caesar, so he set off and finally rescued the foragers, who had been surrounded.

In a much quoted, but pertinent passage, Caesar describes with admiration the way in which the Britons used their war chariots, manned by a driver and a warrior:

> They fight from their chariots in the following manner. First they career in all directions and throw their weapons, and by inspiring terror with the horse teams and the noise of the chariot wheels, they create confusion and panic among the enemy. They work their way into the ranks of the cavalry and the warriors jump down from the chariots and fight on foot, while the drivers move off in the chariots and place them so that the warriors have a means of escape if they are hard-pressed by the enemy. In this way they combine the mobility of cavalry with the stability of infantry, and by daily use and constant practice they become so skilful that they can gallop their horses down the steepest slopes without losing control, swiftly stop and turn them, and the warriors can run along the chariot pole, and stand on the yoke, then dash back into the chariot. (Caesar *Gallic War* 4.33)

A late Roman source insists that the Britons attached scythes to their chariot wheels, and the statue of the British Queen Boudicca on the Thames embankment depicts her in such a vehicle, but the use of scythed wheels is generally discounted by modern historians. Not the least problem would be how to avoid scything down the warriors as well as the enemy, or injuring the horses drawing the other chariots.

Chariot fighting had died out in Gaul, so this was a novelty to the Romans, who were at first thrown into panic. In this instance, Caesar restored calm among the foraging party, but withdrew without trying to fight a pitched battle. He admired the charioteers and the warriors, respecting their skill, and he had to acknowledge that his army was unable to combat this kind of fighting. But by his second expedition he had worked out how to do it.

Clearly a more serious battle was looming, and since the Roman cavalry had failed to arrive, Caesar was hampered in fighting and totally unable to pursue even if he prevailed, because the Britons could get away very quickly in their chariots. When the inevitable battle was joined, he had only thirty horsemen that Commius had brought with him. Caesar describes how he formed up his legions, and won the battle, without elaborating on the details. The Britons came once again suing for peace, so he demanded twice as many hostages as he had asked for previously, and ordered them to be delivered to him in Gaul, where he had always intended to spend the winter. Since the equinox was approaching, with the possibility of storms, he did not want to risk sailing across the Channel with a depleted fleet, and set off back to Gaul as soon as the sea and the weather were calm. When his reports reached Rome, the Senate voted twenty days of thanksgiving for his victory. It all served to keep the distant governor of Gaul in the Roman limelight.

The Second Expedition 54 BC

In planning for his second expedition, Caesar applied the lesson that he had learned from the first. During the winter he had the fleet repaired and had many new ships built, this time to a different design, lower than usual to facilitate loading and disembarking, and making the ships easier to beach. They were also broader than usual, in order to accommodate draught animals. He also wanted sails as well as oars to make the ships more manoeuvrable. In total he had 600 new ships and twenty-eight war galleys, though sixty of these ships were blown off course and never made it to the assembly point, which was once again Portus Itius.

There were delays before Caesar could embark. First he set off to deal with the Treveri, who eventually gave their name to Trier in Germany (the French name for this city being Treves). This tribe ignored Caesar's summons to a council, and Caesar could not be seen to condone such behaviour. Then he summoned chiefs from all the Gallic states, and held some as hostages, also levying 4,000 cavalry from them. Gaul was not quite as peaceful as he had hoped, and he had to take some chieftains with him to Britain to keep an eye on them, and to ensure the good behaviour of their tribesmen. One of the most restive chiefs was Dumnorix of the Aedui, who refused to submit to such treatment, and was held as a captive while preparations were made to set sail. After nearly a whole month of bad weather, at last there was a fair wind, and the fleet was prepared. At this point Dumnorix left the camp, probably thinking that Caesar was too preoccupied to chase after him. But the preparations for embarkation were halted, and some cavalry were sent to bring Dumnorix back, with instructions to kill him if he would not come. He died shouting that he was a free man. Fortunately his tribe remained loyal to the Romans.

Once this bloody episode was over, Caesar put Titus Labienus in command of Gaul, with instructions to guard the ports, and the expedition set sail at sunset, with five legions instead of two this time, and probably 2,000 cavalry, but Caesar only says 'an equal number to those left behind on the continent'. He had given Labienus 2,000 horsemen, so it is likely that he took an equivalent number to Britain.

The ships were blown off course at first, but managed to sail to the landing place that Caesar had used in the previous year, which was, as suggested above, possibly between Deal and Sandwich. The transport ships had to row hard to keep up with the warships, but arrived with the main fleet. Caesar mentions that there were many privately owned ships with his fleet, making about 800 in total, the sight of which convinced the Britons, who had assembled to meet them, that discretion was the better part of valour. They moved away rather than fight on the beaches against such an enormous number of men. Caesar heard of this from some prisoners that he captured. This meant that he would have to go in search of the British warriors, so he made camp, put a guard on the ships, and set off on a night march. He came to a river, probably the Stour, where he found that the Britons had fortified a place nearby, which he says was protected by nature and human engineering, so it sounds like a small hill fort, which archaeologists have suggested may have been at Bigbury, not far from the Stour.

Caesar made another camp, left a guard there, and took the legions to assault the fortifications. Some of the soldiers of the Seventh legion put their shields over their heads and along their sides to form a tortoise (*testudo*) and successfully stormed the place. The Britons fled but Caesar did not pursue them, because he was unsure of the terrain, and had not fortified his own camp properly.

It must have seemed like déjà vu when a message arrived to inform Caesar that the ships had been wrecked once again. Forty of them had been lost. Caesar arrived back at the coast, selected craftsmen from the legions, sent messages to Labienus in Gaul to send tools and equipment, and to build as many ships as he could, as fast as he could. Then the remaining ships were all brought up on shore. If the figures given by Caesar are correct this meant hauling about 760 vessels onto the beach, which would have been an immense task, involving large numbers of men and occupying a very long stretch of the coast. Caesar does not elaborate about the private vessels, how many had been lost, or who was responsible for them. Some of them may have been owned by keen military officers, and others by hangers-on who had come for goods or slaves or other get-rich-quick trading opportunities.

This delay gave the Britons a welcome opportunity to plan what to do next. They sank their differences, collected an army and gave Cassivellaunus the overall command of it. This is the first named individual of the inhabitants of Britain:

> The Britons assembled from all directions, and by common consent they had given the supreme command of the war to Cassivellaunus, whose lands are divided from the coastal zones by the River Thames, about eighty miles from the sea. Before this, there had been continual warfare between this chieftain and the other tribes, but the Britons had been persuaded by our arrival to give him the command for the whole war. (Caesar *Gallic War* 5.11)

Caesar does not provide further information about him, except to say that the British ruler's territory came down to the Thames, which probably means that Cassivellaunus was chief of the Catuvellauni, the tribe that was settled there at a later time, when the Romans began to record lands and tribes.

Cassivellaunus did not seek a major battle with the Romans, but resorted to guerrilla warfare, harassing the cavalry then withdrawing, a ruse which worked well when the Romans pursued too far and found themselves trapped. The Britons used their terrain to good advantage too, hiding in the woods near the place where the Romans were building their camp, and then dashing out to attack. Caesar planted outposts, which received the same treatment. The way in which the Britons fought still perplexed the Romans. They were light armed, nimble and fast moving, and they left groups of warriors all around to form a reserve. These men could preserve their energy and then relieve the fighters as they became exhausted. On one occasion Caesar records how the Britons managed to break through the Roman lines when two legionary cohorts had formed up with a small gap between them, which the Britons exploited. It required infantry and cavalry working together to combat the Britons.

Avoidance of pitched battles was a sensible tactic for Cassivellaunus to adopt, but when three of the Roman legions and all the cavalry went on a foraging expedition, the urge to attack was too strong. Fortunately for the Romans the legions stood their ground and gained the upper hand, repulsed the British tribesmen and the cavalry pursued them as they withdrew. Cassivellaunus never tried to attack the Romans en masse again.

As Caesar advanced towards the River Thames, heading for the one place where it was fordable, the Britons fortified the north bank, placing sharp stakes in the water and along the banks. Nonetheless the legions crossed the river, despite the high water, which was at times up to their necks. They circumvented the man-made obstacles, and drove the Britons off. It is not certain where this confrontation took place, but a case has been made for the area where London was later founded. On his home territory now, Cassivellaunus pruned his warrior band to reduce the number of mouths to feed, keeping 4,000 charioteers, providing mobility and striking power against the Romans wherever they went. He drove off cattle, moved the people away, and scorched the earth to deny the Romans food and fodder. Rather than risking a battle he continued to restrict his attacks to hit and run raids. Caesar responded by keeping his army close together and burning crops and villages.

The tables began to turn when the Trinovantes approached Caesar, offering hostages as a sign of goodwill, and more important, food supplies for the Roman troops. They were no friends of Cassivellaunus, whose expansionist tendencies had made enemies of his neighbours. He had killed the chief of the Trinovantes, as Caesar probably already knew, since the chief's son Mandubracius had come to him in Gaul. With this in mind, it is possible that Caesar had gathered intelligence about the current feelings of the Trinovantes with regard to the Catuvellauni, and had instigated their actions by suggestion, or perhaps something rather less subtle. The tribe asked Caesar to install Mandrubracius as their new chief. In return for their co-operation the Trinovantes were guaranteed protection, not only against other British tribes but against the potential ravages of the Roman troops. There may have been a formal treaty, where the Trinovantes became friends and allies of the Roman people, a political device that bound states or tribes to Rome, but this is to go further than the evidence allows.

Whether or not the Trinovantes entered into a formal agreement, the example spurred other tribes to submit to Caesar, probably because the prospect of prolonged wars and ruined crops was worse than submitting to the Roman leader. Cassivellaunus's days were numbered now that other tribes had gone over to the Romans. Caesar found out where the main British stronghold was situated, and marched there, finding a fortified settlement in woodland, protected by a bank and ditch, with fences constructed from felled trees. It is postulated that this defended site may have been at Wheathampstead. It was probably not a permanent settlement. Strabo describes the fortifications of the Britons:

> The forests are their cities, for they fortify a large circular enclosure
> with felled trees and build huts and pen their cattle, though not for a
> long stay. (Strabo *Geography* 4.5.3)

Caesar says that his troops attacked this fortification from two sides, compelling the Britons to leave rapidly from another side. Cassivellaunus was not yet ready to give up without a fight. He sent word to the four chieftains who ruled in Kent, to ask them to attack the Roman fleet as it lay on the shore, no doubt covering an enormous area that the Romans would probably find difficult to defend. The chieftains responded to Cassivellaunus and attacked, but the legions guarding the ships stood firm and drove the Britons off. After this attack failed, Cassivellaunus probably had no further resources to fall back on.

It was time to come to terms. Commius, the Atrebate chief, acted as intermediary for Cassivellaunus. The terms were light enough, since Caesar was anxious to return to Gaul, as Cassivellaunus probably knew. He had to give hostages, agree to pay an annual tribute to Rome, and make a promise not to harm the Trinovantes, whose lands lay temptingly on his borders. The British chief may have struggled to keep his face straight as he acceded to Caesar's demands, knowing that all he had to do was to wait until Caesar had returned to Gaul, and watch for an opportunity to expand his territory while the Romans were not looking.

Between Caesar and Claudius

An unanswerable question concerns Caesar's ultimate intentions for Britain. He may have considered a full scale conquest, converting the whole island into another province when he had subdued the whole of Gaul. It has been pointed out that the language that he uses in describing his arrangements with the chiefs is diplomatic and official, as though he thought of his expeditions as more than just exploratory adventures designed to glorify his name, and may have intended to utilise the agreements he had made as the first stages in annexation. On the other hand it is likely that he did not consider splitting hairs over terminology, using words that the Romans would understand, and at the same time leaving his options open. Nothing came of any designs he may have had on Britain. The historian Tacitus says that Caesar revealed Britain to the Romans, but did not bequeath it. After the conquest of Gaul, Caesar had no time to turn to Britain. He became immediately involved in civil war with his erstwhile ally, Pompey the Great, and shortly after the final victory against the Pompeians in Africa and Spain, he was assassinated in 44 BC. For the next fourteen years the Romans fought each other, until in 30 BC Octavian emerged victorious over Antony and Cleopatra, his last rivals for sole power.

It is not known whether the tribute that Caesar had asked for was ever paid. There are hints in the work of Strabo that it had ceased, but the Romans were more than compensated by customs dues, without the bother and fuss of conquering, annexing, garrisoning and administering the island:

> At the moment more revenue is gained from customs duties than tribute could bring in, if you deduct the cost of the forces that would be needed to garrison the country and collect the tribute. (Strabo *Geography* 5.8)

Tribesmen were generally more comfortable making an agreement with a leader or ruler, as opposed to a state, and the agreement was often considered still valid for the leader's heirs, so for a while the Britons perhaps did pay their annual tribute to Rome, especially when Octavian/Augustus became the heir of Caesar. The general assumption, however, is that the tribute levied by Julius Caesar ceased at some point. In Rome there seems to have been no public outcry against the Britons for defaulting on their agreement, which would have made a reasonable excuse for another expedition to reinforce the demands. This may be what lies behind Dio's statements indicating that on three occasions in 34, 27 and 26 BC, Augustus did prepare for war against the Britons. On the first occasion, no motive is listed, but for the second and third abortive campaigns, a reason for concern is given, albeit somewhat vague. Augustus reached Gaul in 27 BC, but stayed there because there was considerable unrest in the province, and in any case it seemed that the Britons were suddenly willing to come to terms. These terms are unfortunately not outlined, nor is there any further enlightenment when Dio says that in the following year Augustus was anxious for war in Britain because the people would not come to terms, which implies that demands had been made in 27 BC, and the Britons had prolonged the discussions, then finally refused to meet the demands, which may well have been made for the payment of tribute as agreed with Caesar. Perhaps this problem was put on the back burner until a suitable opportunity presented itself. In the literature of the Augustan age, the eventual conquest of the island was taken for granted, at least in the early part of Augustus's reign.

Although he may have planned to invade Britain if opportunity arose, Augustus never did so. As mentioned above there were three separate occasions when a campaign might have been mounted, but nothing came of them. Augustus was presented with further excuses to invade when two British chiefs came to him to ask for help in fighting off their enemies, but although he records the events in his account of his achievements during his reign, the *Res Gestae*, or literally 'things done', he never rose to the bait. The full name of one of these British rulers is lost, surviving only as Tin…, previously restored as Tincommius, supposedly a son or a descendant of Commius of the Atrebates. More recently coins have been discovered in Atrebate territory in Hampshire, with the name Tincomarus, which is the most likely restoration of the name in the *Res Gestae*. The other chief was Dubnovellaunus, ruler of the Trinovantes.

The arrival of these two British chiefs is not dated in Augustus's memoir of his achievements. They may not have arrived both at the same time, and it can only be surmised that they came, individually or in tandem, sometime after 30 BC when Antony and Cleopatra were defeated, and Octavian became sole ruler of the whole Roman world, though he did not publicise his achievements in such a blatant way. It is thought that the *Res Gestae* was composed at some point before AD 7, so somewhere between these two dates of 30 BC and AD 7, the British tribal chiefs were clearly having trouble keeping their lands and rule intact. It may be that Dio's account of abortive preparations for a British campaign in 27 and 26 BC are contemporary with the flight of the two British chiefs, but there is no proof. It seems that there had been some sort of dialogue with the Britons at that time, which may have concerned the tribute that Caesar had levied, and/or an attempt to force the Catuvellauni to honour their promise not to harass the Trinovantes.

The Trinovantes and the Atrebates were neighbours of the Catuvellauni, now one of the most powerful tribes in Britain, with the most aggressive expansionist policies. Catuvellaunian rule extended from the Thames into Northamptonshire, and they seemed keen to gather more lands. By 15 BC a chieftain called Tasciovanus had succeeded Cassivellaunus, whose date of death is not known. Tasciovanus may have been his grandson. More crucial than his precise family relationship to the previous rulers was the fact that

Tasciovanus had started to issue coins, and some of them have been found in Essex. The appearance of coins may mean nothing more than gift exchange or trade, but some of Tasciovanus's Catuvellaunian coins have mint marks from Colchester, so it would seem that at an unknown date he had taken over the capital of the Trinovantes. He was succeeded by Cunobelinus, perhaps the most famous British tribal ruler, known to the Elizabethans and Shakespeare as Cymbeline. Coins of Cunobelinus bear the Latin legend TASC.FIL, or in its expanded form *Tasciovani filius*, son of Tasciovanus, indicating that although Cunobelinus may not have been a natural son, he was designated heir and successor of Tasciovanus. He was a worthy choice, if strong rule and an appetite for expansion were required, and he seems to have exercised this appetite without opposition from Rome, despite the fact that Tasciovanus and then he himself had breached the agreement with Caesar to leave the Trinovantes in peace.

After Caesar's invasions, several tribes were still in contact with Rome, according to Strabo:

Some of the chiefs of the Britons have secured the friendship of Caesar Augustus through their embassies and by paying court to him. They have made votive offerings on the Capitol Hill and have almost made the whole island Roman property. (Strabo *Geography* 4.5.3)

The Trinovantes were among those who retained their allegiance to Rome. Remains of Italian wine amphorae are regularly found in their territory, most especially in their tombs. Their contact with Rome may have been limited to trading activities, but it was enough to ensure that they remembered the Romans and knew where to turn for help. Similarly the Atrebates retained contact with Rome. They issued coins from their capital at Silchester, with Latin words and Roman forms, probably produced by Roman die cutters and mint workers, which suggests that close diplomatic contacts had been formed between the tribal leaders and Rome. After about 16 BC Roman imports began to pour into Atrebate territory.

It is suggested that the Atrebate leader Tincomarus may have been eventually ousted by his brother Epillus, who was succeeded after only a short time by another brother, Verica. These last two Atrebate rulers issued coins on which they called themselves *Rex*, Latin for king. This may simply mean that they had adopted Roman terminology to describe their ruling status, but some authors have seen this as confirmation that they were officially recognised as 'friends of the Roman people' or client kings as modern historians label them. It was a system that the Romans regularly adopted, where the native ruling elite were offered protection in return for keeping their own people under control, and sometimes they were obliged to contribute men for the Roman army. Gifts from the Romans, and trading rights with Rome were often part of the package, usually sealed by an official arrangement or treaty. This may be to read far too much into the use of the title *Rex* on British coins, which perhaps held no connotations whatsoever of a Roman alliance. Whatever the true relationship of the Atrebates to Rome, their growing imports of luxury goods may have attracted the Catuvellauni. Coins of Cunobelinus have been found at the Atrebate settlement at Silchester. Around the same time Cunobelinus started to mint coins at Verulamium. Control of trading ventures may have been one of the foremost reasons for extending Catuvellaunian dominance over neighbouring lands and people.

Once they had installed themselves in Colchester, the Catuvellauni provided their settlement with defensive rectilinear ditches, surrounding the site known to archaeologists as Sheepen Farm. It is thought the earlier capital of the Trinovantes lay some short distance away at Gosbeck's Farm, where curvilinear ditches have been found. The finds at the Sheepen site show that the Catuvellauni developed an almost insatiable desire for Roman goods. Amphorae carrying oil and wine are abundant, and good Roman pottery and metalwork are found in quantity, possibly arriving with shiploads of more perishable luxuries which have not survived. Most of the items were brought from Italy, but some hailed from Gaul, or Spain.

The potential power that control of trade would bring may have been what brought the Cautvellauni to the Trinovantian capital in the first place, rather than a desire for territorial conquest which just happened to give them a lucrative spin-off by way of imports. By the first century AD they were importing a broader range of goods, and the spread of these items widened, covering a larger area. It may be that the Catuvellauni were entrepreneurs in trade themselves, since the Dobunni, further to the west, clearly liked the pottery that they made, but these tribesmen also began to import other commodities that may have come through the hands of enterprising Catuvellaunian traders. Colchester would be an excellent centre to bring in goods for home use, or for redistribution.

The obvious importance of trade with the Britons of the south and south-east, which seems to have operated on a large scale, raises the question of how it was organised. Once the goods had arrived at a tribal centre, the native leaders themselves could have arranged for the redistribution for profit or for gift exchange, but the sheer quantity of goods inwards suggests that somewhere on the coasts and river estuaries there were regular dealers and shippers who brought cargoes of Roman goods in and shipped a return cargo of British goods out. There is evidence of a trading depot at Poole harbour, which perhaps came into being as the port at Hengistbury Head declined, but it is postulated that other sites further to the east may have been established, especially along the Thames, where Roman dealers, not necessarily from the city of Rome, perhaps set up trading centres. These may one day come to light via archaeological research.

Strabo's assertion that the British willingly paid their customs dues on imports implies that there was an organised collection process, perhaps with Roman officials at the points of delivery and disembarkation. How did the Britons pay their tribute, or their customs dues? In Caesar's day, before the British rulers had started to mint coins on a regular basis, tribute may have been levied in kind, probably in the form of grain, or slaves. Customs dues may have been paid by the same methods, rather than in coin, though by the early first century AD the Romans had found out that there were deposits of silver in the island, and they were mining for it within a very short time after the conquest under Claudius in AD 43. If the pre-conquest system of collection of customs dues embraced payment in kind, there would be a need for Roman officials to assess the amounts to be levied, to ensure that they equalled the relevant percentage of the value of goods inwards.

When Caesar entered his province of Gaul in 58 BC, the future connection between Britain and Rome was assured. Even if he had never set foot in the island, the Romanisation of the whole province of Gaul, only a few short miles away from Britain over the Channel, would have affected the tribes of the south and south-east in some way, if only on the basis of increased trade and a knowledge of the powerful state of Rome, where assistance could be obtained in cases of internal warfare of external threat. As it was, Caesar's expeditions had served to highlight these factors, and also to show that despite contrary winds and Channel tides it was possible to land an army there. As early as Augustus's reign, ejected British rulers tried to persuade the Romans to help reinstate them, just as rulers of tribes all around the Empire knew where to turn for assistance. Probably in AD 39, Adminius, the son of Cunobelin, turned up at the court of Caligula, because he had been exiled from the kingdom, and at best he hoped for Roman intervention, or at worst, sanctuary for himself. Caligula may have considered mounting an expedition to Britain. He appeared in Gaul with troops, as though to prepare for an invasion, but there was an incursion of the Germans across the Rhine, and the only achievement with slight regard to Britain was the building of a lighthouse at Boulogne.

In the following year, or at least before AD 43, it is thought that Cunobelin died, succeeded by his sons Caratacus and Togodumnus. Under their rule the Catuvellauni probably took advantage of internal squabbles among the Atrebates to infiltrate their territory. According to Dio, a British chief called Bericus arrived at Claudius's court in AD 43. His name is usually given as Verica, who may have been overthrown by the Catuvellauni, though opinion is divided on the reason why he fled to Rome. When he did so, he perhaps did not anticipate that the response to his request for help would result in the Roman occupation of Britain for nearly four hundred years.

2

Invasion & Conquest
AD 43 to 60

Claudius Becomes Emperor

Immediately after the assassination of the infamous Emperor Caligula in AD 41, his uncle Claudius, hitherto considered an unimportant member of the Julio-Claudian family because of his lameness and his speech impediment, was found hiding behind a curtain by the German Imperial bodyguard, who proclaimed him the next Emperor. Claudius was reluctant to take on the government of the Empire, but was given little choice in the matter except to accede to the wishes of the bodyguard, or perhaps be run through with a couple of swords while the soldiers went off to search for someone else to proclaim, thus ensuring that in having someone to guard they still had jobs and pay packets.

Claudius had grown up through the reigns of the first three Emperors. As a child he had witnessed the later years of Augustus's reign, and had lived through the whole reigns of Tiberius and Caligula. He was related to them all by blood or by marriage. His father was Nero Claudius Drusus Germanicus, the second son of Livia by her first husband, before she married the rising politician Octavian/Augustus. Livia's family connections were helpful to Octavian, who also attempted to manipulate the political future of the Roman Republic by arranging a marriage between his sister Octavia and Mark Antony. Claudius's mother was their younger daughter, Antonia.

Born in 10 BC at Lugdunum (modern Lyon), Claudius was scarcely one year old when his father, campaigning against the Germans, had a serious fall from his horse, damaging his leg. He lived long enough to say farewell to his elder brother, the future Emperor Tiberius, who travelled from Rome to the German frontier in record time to see him. The military achievements of these two brothers, Tiberius and Nero Drusus, were legendary, and though Claudius had little chance to witness their exploits for himself, he would be aware of their joint reputation, which contrasted sharply with his own lack of experience. Barred from many aspects of political life, except for holding token appointments under Augustus and Caligula, and totally excluded from any hope of army command, Claudius had become a scholarly recluse, but his years of study were of great use to him as Emperor.

The expansion of the Roman Empire stagnated after the disaster in Germany in AD 9, when three Roman legions under the governor Quinctilius Varus were wiped out by the supposedly pacified German tribes. Augustus died five years later, advising his successor Tiberius to leave the boundaries as they were, and not to try to gain territory beyond them. Tiberius had spent most of his life at the head of armies, fighting battles on behalf of his stepfather Augustus on the northern frontiers, and was only too happy to give up warfare and attend to government and administration. His relationship with the Senate and people of Rome was not a happy one, and despite his efforts to improve this relationship he soon withdrew from public life as much as possible, eventually retiring to the island of Capri. Tiberius left many of the provincial governors in their posts for several years, so that the paths to promotion became somewhat clogged. No one was going anywhere, except the notorious Praetorian Prefect Lucius Aelius Sejanus, to whom Tiberius delegated most of the affairs of state. Sejanus quickly took advantage of the freedom that he was allowed, and instituted a reign of terror in Tiberius's name. His lust for power was limitless. He even tried to ally himself to the Imperial family by marriage, but was rebuffed. Only one person, Claudius's mother Antonia, had the courage to denounce Sejanus and explain to Tiberius that the Praetorian Prefect was all powerful in Rome. Tiberius arranged for the execution of Sejanus by the other Praetorian Prefect, Sutorius Macro.

Tiberius died aged seventy-eight in AD 37, succeeded by his great nephew Gaius, more popularly known as Caligula. His reign was disastrous but mercifully short, ending with his assassination in AD 41, when Claudius, nephew of Tiberius and uncle of Caligula, became Emperor against his will. He took his role seriously, expressing perhaps too much interest in the finicky details of government, legal affairs, and the welfare of the people, not just with regard to the Romans or Italians, but also the provincials of the growing Empire. He had undoubted ability, but he lacked military experience, and wished to share in the glory that conquest of new areas could bring him and the Romans. The project of Britain had been one of the main literary themes of the early years of Augustus's reign, and Claudius would have read the works of the poets and historians who constantly kept the theme alive. In Tiberius's reign the projected conquest of Britain may have sunk into the background, but under Caligula it had revived, briefly, when the British chief Adminius appeared at the Imperial court, having been exiled by his father Cunobelinus. Then, barely two years after Claudius had become Emperor, Verica, ruler of the Atrebates, arrived from Britain, seeking help to regain power in his kingdom.

The Matter of Britain

Claudius's desire for military glory is often quoted as the reason for his invasion of Britain, but other considerations may have influenced his decision to conquer the island. Although Strabo said that the cost of garrisoning Britain would probably outweigh the potential profits, nearly one hundred years of trading with the tribes of the south and south-east had revealed what might be possible if the area of trading activities could be extended. Britain yielded metals, tin and copper in the south-west, iron ore in the Weald and the Forest of Dean, lead and potentially silver in the Mendips and the Pennines, and in Wales there was gold. Strabo list the principal exports from Britain:

> [The island] produces grain, cattle, gold, silver and iron, which are exported along with hides, slaves and dogs specifically bred for hunting. (Strabo *Geography* 4.5.2)

From the sea there was a reliable crop of oysters and their pearls, though Tacitus scoffs at their low quality. In the north, the natives raised cattle, which would be a source not only of meat but hides, as listed by Strabo. Hides were always of supreme importance to the Roman army, so much so that the taxes levied from the Friesian tribes consisted mostly of leather. All these economic factors will have been considered by the Emperor Claudius, but in the absence of a written treatise from the Emperor himself, setting out his thoughts on Britain, speculation is the only tool with which to judge the motives for his enterprise.

Time and manpower were available for this new project. Gaius had created two extra legions and placed them on the Rhine. By this time, the German tribes were slightly less hostile, and their warrior skills had been turned to the benefit of the Empire as the tribesmen were recruited for the Roman army. The potential threat to the provinces bordering on the Rhine and Danube had diminished, so there were now large numbers of soldiers who could be considered superfluous to the defence of the areas where they were stationed. Julius Caesar had shown that an invasion across the Channel from Gaul was feasible, though if he had ever intended to annex Britain he had not been granted the time, and had therefore revealed only a small part of the island in the south and south-east.

Uncertainty about what they might encounter in the rest of Britain may be the reason why the troops that Claudius assembled in Gaul initially refused to embark. Knowledge of the tribes beyond the Catuvellauni was probably sparse, and though the Romans called Britain an island, it was not yet known for certain what happened in the furthest northern parts of it. There was probably a suspicion among the troops that anyone venturing that far would fall off the edge of the world. Another consideration is that the legionaries who took part in Julius Caesar's expedition knew they were to go back to Gaul for the winter, but the soldiers of Claudius's army were to be permanently uprooted and sent into what they probably regarded as exile. So they decided that they were not going.

Among Claudius's intimate staff was his secretary, Narcissus, an ex-slave but now undoubtedly powerful within the Imperial household and a good man to know if you wanted to get on in life. Narcissus was sent to speak to the troops. According to Dio he was not allowed to utter a word, but one of the soldiers, copied by others, shouted '*Io Saturnalia*', referring to the winter festival of role-reversal, when the slaves of a household were given a meal served by their masters. The legions and auxiliaries embarked.

The commander of the British expedition was Aulus Plautius, whose family had been allies of the Claudians for some time. Claudius's first wife, Urgulanilla, was a member of the family of the Plautii, and though it was not a successful match, the two families remained allies. Aulus Plautius had been consul in AD 29, but as suffect consul for only a few months, rather than one of the *consules ordinarii*, who gave their name to the year. The system of appointing a pair of suffect consuls, or several pairs, who took over government as the preceding pair stepped down, enabled a greater number of senators to gain some experience of government, and the appointment then qualified them for other civil posts, or for military commands. By AD 42, Plautius was the governor of Pannonia, where the IX Hispana legion was based. He brought it with him for the British expedition.

The other legions known to have formed the invasion force were II Augusta from Strasbourg, XIV Gemina from Mainz, and the XX legion from Neuss. These last two legions did not yet have their respective titles Martia Victrix and Valeria Victrix, which were awarded after the suppression of the rebellion under Boudicca in AD 60 or 61. Although it is known which legions took part in the conquest of Britain, the exact numbers of men in Claudius's invasion army cannot be established beyond a rough estimate. If each legion contained 5,000 men, this would give a paper-strength of 20,000 soldiers, but it is not known whether some men may have been left behind in the original bases until the troops of the Rhine and Danube were reshuffled. Similarly it is not know how many auxiliary troops accompanied the legions. Despite the unknown and probably unanswerable questions about the numbers of men, it is usually estimated that the invasion force for Britain totalled about 40,000 troops. This is assuming that there were only four legions in the invasion force. On very slender evidence, it is suggested that there may have been another legion, or at least a detachment (vexillation) from it, VIII Augusta from Strasbourg. This assumption derives from an inscription from Turin naming the patron of the town, the veteran soldier Gaius Gavius Silanus, *primus pilus*, literally 'first spear' or chief centurion, of VIII Augusta. The inscription says that he was highly decorated by Claudius in the British war, receiving torques, armbands, and *phalerae* (metal discs to be displayed over the armour on the chest), and the supreme honour of the *corona aurea*, or golden crown. Unfortunately the inscription does not give any details about Gaius Gavius's exploits in Britain. One inscription cannot be taken as proof that the whole of the legion named on it was in Britain during the invasion, and it is notable that the text mentions only the higher ranking posts that Gavius held, starting with his appointment as *primus pilus* in VIII Augusta, and then as tribune of three units in Rome, first the *Vigiles*, then the Urban Cohorts, and finally the Praetorian Guard. This could indicate that Gavius had served in other legions in a lesser capacity, perhaps as centurion, and that it was his brave deeds in Britain, possibly while he served in one of the four legions there, that helped to gain promotion for him in other units.

The Imperial Roman Army

The Roman legions were all given numbers, but the system can be confusing. Some legions were allocated their numbers during the Republic, but although there was an army in the field on an almost permanent basis, there was no standing army and troops could be disbanded after a campaign ended. There was never a logical numbering procedure whereby successive numbers were allocated to each legion as it was formed. At the end of the civil wars, Augustus drastically pruned the number of legions that he inherited, and out of the remainder, about twenty-eight legions, he created the standing army. Numbering did not start afresh from I to XXVIII, since the older legions, formed under Caesar or Mark Antony or Augustus himself, retained their original numbers. This entailed some duplication, so that there were, eventually, no less than six legions with the number I, six more with the number II, five numbered III, and so on. Their descriptive names, such as Augusta, Hispana, Alaudae and Ferrata, serve to distinguish them from each other. However, there seems to have been only one XX legion, and after the Claudian conquest it spent its life in Britain.

Only Roman citizens could serve in the legions, but this does not mean that all the men came from Rome, since Roman citizenship had been awarded to Italians, and then to some provincials. The smallest unit within a legion was the century, commanded by a centurion and his second-in-command, the *optio*. The terminology implies that there were a hundred men in a century but the full complement was eighty men, based on the tent group (*contubernium*) of eight men. Six centuries of eighty men and their officers were grouped together to make one cohort, but there is no evidence to suggest that there was a cohort commander, so responsibility for routine organisation and discipline in peacetime, and action in battle, rested with the centurions. Ten cohorts made up one legion, though in some legions, if not all of them, the first century was of double strength. These figures allow historians to work out an approximation of how many men there would be in a legion, somewhere between five and six thousand. This is all that can be said, since no contemporary Roman or Greek source outlines the number of men in a legion, and it is not known if the legions were all of a standard size.

The men who commanded the legions were senators who had experience of both military operations and of civilian government. The Roman career path, or *cursus honorum*, embraced all kinds of appointments, mixing administrative posts with army ones. The legionary legates (*legati legionis*) of the Empire were appointed by the Emperor, and often stayed in post for about three years. They could look forward to further appointments, for example as governors of a civil province which contained no troops, then perhaps election to the consulship.

Second-in-command of the legion was the *tribunus laticlavius* or 'broad stripe' tribune. The broad stripe on the toga indicated senatorial status, but the young men who were appointed as *tribuni laticlavii* had not yet become senators, although they were drawn from the senatorial class. After one year or more of military service these young officers customarily embarked on a series of administrative posts in Rome or the provinces. It was usual for young men to enter the Senate after an appointment as quaestor, and after serving in a variety of several civilian and military posts some of them could look forward to an appointment as legionary legate.

The camp prefect (*praefectus castrorum*) was third-in-command of the legion. He was usually a career soldier who had served as a centurion, working his way up to the post of senior centurion (*primus pilus*, or 'first spear') of the first cohort, which as mentioned above was usually if not always of double strength. The camp prefects were not from the senatorial class, but from the middle classes, or equestrians, who ranked below the senators. Lack of senatorial status did not stultify their careers, however, since there were always good prospects for promotion for men who had been camp prefects. A fortunate few could be promoted to the Praetorian Guard, or occasionally as procurators looking after financial affairs in the provinces.

Other officers in the legion included the *tribuni angusticlavii* or 'narrow stripe' tribunes, indicating that they were not senators but equestrians. These young men were usually at the beginning of their careers. There were five of these tribunes in each legion, with varied duties which could include taking command of detachments of legionaries. Since there were no military academies or staff colleges where such men could be taught the business of command, they presumably relied upon knowledge gained from military manuals, of which some survive, and from advice from family, friends and fellow officers. The centurions were the men who really counted, to both the senior officers and to the serving soldiers. Since they could make life for the ordinary soldiers either miserable or bearable, as they wished, they had to be appeased and often bribed, for instance when a soldier applied for leave. Centurions were of mixed origin, some being career soldiers, while others may have been appointed simply by asking influential friends for a posting. Military experience was not a necessary attribute for officers and commanders. Nevertheless the Roman army generally functioned reasonably well.

In addition to the legions the Romans recruited units of *auxilia*, literally 'help troops'. The auxiliary soldiers were not Roman citizens, and in Claudius's day these units were still undergoing the final stages of their development. Under the older Republican arrangements, native warriors were engaged to fight alongside the legions, usually under their own native commanders, for the duration of the war. Under the Empire, the auxiliary units were converted into regular formations of the Roman army, comprising non-citizen soldiers commanded by Roman officers. On completion of twenty-five years service the auxiliaries were rewarded with Roman citizenship, which at first extended to their children, but the privilege of enfranchisement for all the soldier's offspring was withdrawn by the Emperor Antoninus Pius, and granted only to the children born after the soldier received his citizenship.

The auxiliaries were organised as cavalry units (*alae*), infantry units (*cohortes*) or mixed cavalry and infantry (*cohortes equitatae*). The majority of these cohorts were 500-strong (quingenary), but a proportion of all three types of auxiliary units were 1,000-strong (milliary). The milliary cavalry units were rare, usually restricted to only one in each province. Commanders of auxiliary units were Roman officers, called prefects in the quingenary units, and tribunes in the milliary ones. They were all from the equestrian class, with genuine promotion prospects as they worked their way up through the various units.

The Invasion

The main sources of information about the course of the invasion and the first years of the Roman conquest derive from Dio. The historian Tacitus did cover the subject, but the relevant parts of his work have been lost, a great misfortune, since he wrote at the end of the first century, and was consequently writing about comparatively recent history – and he could check his facts with people who remembered the events. He also had the great advantage of inside knowledge about Britain, having married the daughter of Gnaeus Julius Agricola, who served as tribune in one of the legions of Britain during the rebellion of Boudicca, subsequently commanded the XX legion as legate sometime later, and went on to become governor of the island from *c*.AD 77 to *c*.AD 84.

In the absence of Tacitus's account, historians have to rely on Cassius Dio, whose Roman history was written in the early third century. It is judged by many scholars to be fairly reliable, since Dio seems to have used equally reliable sources, including official records. Apart from the rhetoric that he invents, like all ancient authors, for the speeches delivered by his main characters, the events that he relates are probably not too far from the truth. Unfortunately, his wording does not always guarantee clarity, especially at a remove of nearly twenty centuries. For instance, when Dio says that Plautius invaded Britain in three waves, so as to avoid the potential opposition that a single force may have encountered, it is not certain whether he means that there were three successive sailings and landings in the same location, or whether there were three simultaneous landings at three different places. If there was only one location for disembarking, this was almost certainly at Richborough. From there, the Romans could access the Thames easily, and buildings of Claudian date have been detected on the site. Furthermore Richborough was later used as one of the main entry points to Britain, and a huge arch was built, foursquare, massive and designed to impress. If there were other landing places, only guesswork can tentatively identify them. Dover and Lympne have been suggested, and also possibly Fishbourne, because it lay in the friendly territory of the Atrebates. One day, archaeological finds may prove where the Roman forces landed and made their first camps.

The first possibility, of three waves landing in succession, implies that one third of the force would have to gain a foothold to allow the others to come up safely, and the alternative interpretation, of three different groups using separate landing places suggests that the whole army would have to join up somewhere, and run the risk of being defeated piecemeal before it had done so. In the end, though, none of this applied, because there were no Britons to fight. It was said that they did not believe that the Romans would arrive. Dio's Britons are not like Caesar's. They keep on being taken by surprise, though Dio does mention marshes and woods, which the Britons relied upon for their version of guerrilla warfare.

Plautius went to look for the Britons, and defeated the Catuvellaunian leaders, Caratacus and Togodumnus, separately. There is a frustrating lack of detail in Dio's laconic account, with no indication of where these battles were fought. As a result of these victories, Plautius received the submission of a tribe that Dio calls the Bodunni, usually (but not universally) taken to be the Dobunni, who had been subject to the Catuvellauni.

The next scene takes place at a river crossing, where the Britons camped on the opposite bank, secure in their conviction that the Romans would not be able to cross, but they had reckoned without the Celtic warriors among the army, who were trained to swim across such obstacles in full armour. Dio gives no tribal name or military unit for these so-called Celts, so it is tempting, if rash, to link them with the Batavian units who swam across the River Po near Placentia some years later, during the civil wars of AD 69, but it is not known if any such units were in Britain as early as AD 43.

The Britons were surprised by these aquatic warriors, whoever they were, and they were even more disturbed when the Celts used their arrows to bring down the horses of the chariots, removing the possibility of a quick getaway. Even so, the British warriors gave as good as they got, and Plautius sent over more troops under Titus Flavius Vespasianus and his brother Sabinus. The legionary commander Vespasianus became more familiarly known, twenty-seven years in the future, as the Emperor Vespasian.

The action broke off for the night, but it was not yet a victory, because the Britons attacked again next day, surrounding and nearly capturing an officer called Gnaeus Hosidius Geta, but under his direction the Romans rallied and drove the Britons off. Geta was awarded *ornamenta triumphalia*, the highest distinction for Roman officers, the insignia of a triumph for military exploits. In Republican times he would have been awarded a real triumph in Rome, to parade through the streets and dedicate the spoils of war to Jupiter in the temple on the Capitoline Hill. During the later Republic the state had been disrupted by generals whose successes in warfare, and concomitant command of soldiers who were loyal to them rather than to the government, had led some of them to make a bid for supremacy. Augustus himself had risen to power in this way, but in order to retain his position as head of state he could not allow any of his generals to rise too high, so he put a stop to any overt display of power. The triumph was the most overt display of all, and so it was restricted to immediate members of the Imperial family. In the place of an actual triumph, the *ornamenta triumphalia* conferred the supreme distinction on successful generals, without the pomp and ceremony or the potential for inflaming the populace.

After their defeat in this second battle, the Britons drew off to the Thames, which Dio actually names. The Britons, knowing their terrain, chose a place near the point where the river flows into the sea, where a lake was formed at high tide. It is suggested that this may have been at London. Once again the Celts crossed the river, and some troops used a bridge further upstream, which does not seem to have been defended. In the ensuing battle the Britons fled, but they knew their way across the marshes, and the pursuing Romans did not, so the Britons got away and the Romans were bogged down, with many losses. The subsequent fate of the Britons is unknown. Caratacus fled westwards, turning up sometime later as a leader of the Silures and Ordovices in Wales. For unexplained reasons, his brother Togodumnus died, or was killed. The Catuvellauni were now without a leader, and there is no information to suggest whether they appointed one. The Romans were poised for the final attack on the tribal headquarters at Camulodunum, modern Colchester. And at this point, Plautius called a halt. It was said that he had been instructed to send for Claudius if he met with difficulty, so that the Emperor could sweep into Britain and then be seen to be the fearless leader of the Roman army. It is more likely that he and Plautius had agreed that the Imperial household should be summoned when the fruit was ripe for picking, so to speak.

It is not known what Plautius did in the interval between calling a halt and the arrival of Claudius. Presumably he made camps, consolidated what he had gained so far, put out feelers to the other tribes to test their reactions, possibly forming alliances to be ratified by Claudius himself. As soon as the Emperor received the news, he placed his fellow consul Lucius Vitellius in command during his absence, and set out with all haste from Rome. He sailed down the Tiber to Ostia, took ship for Marseilles, crossed Gaul by land and water transport, and embarked for Britain. He had already made preparations for this part of the expedition. In order to impress the Britons, he had even assembled some elephants, which was perhaps not something that could be arranged on a whim at short notice.

Once he had joined the army, Claudius made straight for the Catuvellaunian capital, going for the jugular, as it were. The battle was a resounding success. Claudius was hailed by the troops as Imperator several times, a most unusual circumstance for a single short campaign. The spontaneous acclamation of the soldiers for a successful general had its roots in Republican times, and the Emperors zealously collected these honours, numbering them on inscriptions in abbreviated form, as IMP I or IMP II and so on. Claudius was already IMP III at the beginning of 43, and had collected another twelve salutations by 47 when Plautius was succeeded as governor by Ostorius Scapula. Claudius's final total was twenty-seven Imperial salutations, an unprecedented number, especially for a man who had little or no experience of military service until late in life.

A fortunate result of the Emperor's success in Britain was the voluntary submission of eleven tribes under their various rulers. This achievement was evidently very important to Claudius. According to the biographer Suetonius, the Emperor put on displays in the Campus Martius in Rome, recreating the storming of a town, with actors playing the parts of the British kings who submitted to the Emperor, in a Roman parallel to the drama-documentaries that are frequently broadcast to modern audiences on television. The event is also recorded on a fragmentary inscription found in Rome, from the triumphal arch that Claudius set up, probably dating to AD 51 or 52. The text specifically mentions REGES BRIT, and a fragment records the number XI, eleven British kings. As one scholar famously remarked, it has never been more difficult to choose a British first eleven. Only a few of the tribes are identifiable. King Prasutagus of the Iceni, who were neighbours of the Catuvellauni in what was to become East Anglia, was no doubt one of these allied rulers, since the Iceni were described as such under the next governor, Ostorius Scapula. The Brigantes of the north, ruled by Queen Cartimandua, are also presumed to have made an alliance with the Romans. It is to be expected that the Atrebates were counted among the allies, though nothing is known of what happened to their ruler Verica, who had sought Claudius's help. Verica disappears from the record without trace, just as his probable successor Tiberius Claudius Togidubnus enters it, fully fledged with no known past history.

Togidubnus is the most famous of the allies who submitted to Claudius. His name is sometimes rendered as Togidumnus, or Togodumnus, or even Cogidubnus, or Cogidumnus, all of these versions being forms of the Latin construction of a British name, where the sounds for 'b' and 'm' were interchangeable. Connection with Caratacus's brother of similar name is unlikely and cannot be demonstrated. Togidubnus's full Romanised name indicates that Claudius had bestowed Roman citizenship on him, and in accordance with usual practice, Togidubnus took the names of the man who had enfranchised him. This was a signal honour for a British ruler so early in the conquest, but unfortunately we do not know the circumstances of the grant of citizenship, nor is it possible to say where Togidubnus had come from.

According to Tacitus, several *civitates*, states or tribes, were grouped together by the Romans and installed under the rule of Togidubnus, though it is not known which tribes were incorporated into his new kingdom. They were eventually merged to become a single tribe called the Regnenses, the people of the *Regnum* or kingdom of Togidubnus. Tacitus says that the king remained loyal to the Romans up to recent times that he himself could remember.

Togidubnus is named in full on an inscription found in the early eighteenth century at Chichester. The inscription is damaged, and for several years the text was interpreted as R[EX] LEG. AUG. IN B[RITANNIA]. This would mean that Togidubnus was king and also a *legatus Augusti*, a legate of the Emperor in Britain. Cultivation of the elite was normal, but elevating them to such high rank and bestowing office on them was not. More recently, another much closer look at the stone and its damaged text has resulted in a more acceptable interpretation of Togidubnus as REX MAGNUS, or great king, which was a formula used for those client kings who allied with Rome and ruled over more than one area or tribe. This fits the bill much more easily, corroborated by Tacitus's statement that Togidubnus was ruler of several *civitates*. It has been suggested that Togidubnus was the occupant of the first buildings on the site of what would become the truly lavish palace at Fishbourne, though this remains a theory. Someone of tremendous importance obviously lived in this early villa, not yet a palace, but it is not certain whether this may have been a Roman official. In his rule over different tribes, whoever they were, Togidubnus perhaps used more than one centre, in the territory of each of his subject peoples. Presumably while he remained loyal to the Romans, so did the tribesmen, but this is not necessarily the case.

It is not known under what terms the British kings submitted to Claudius. There may not have been an entirely standard formula for all the tribes, but perhaps the arrangements were tailored to circumstances. There would be legal agreements about obligations to be observed, territorial boundaries to be established, all of which would probably be more favourable to the Romans than the natives. In theory, the Romans were the protectors of the tribes who had submitted. Modern historians refer to the rulers of such allied states as client kings.

Client Kings

'Client king' is a modern term invented by historians to describe the relationship between Rome and those rulers who had chosen to enter into the formal arrangement which recognised them as friends and allies of the Roman people. The precise formula was *rex sociusque et amicus*, king and ally and friend, each term outlining their status, king in their own territory, and an ally and friend of the Romans, which meant that they must have the same friends and enemies as the Romans, and could not ally with any other power unless the agreement was sanctioned by Rome. Client kings were not entirely free after coming to an arrangement with Rome.

There was some formality in granting client status to a king and his people, often accompanied by grand ceremonial after the Senate had decreed formal acceptance. The initiative for seeking such acceptance usually came from the ruler and his tribe or state, rather than through Roman compulsion. Cleopatra, for instance, was determined to achieve such recognition after the death of her father, Ptolemy Auletes, because it meant that she would receive Roman protection for herself and her regime, and by such means she could perhaps forestall Roman schemes for the outright annexation of Egypt, at least for her lifetime if not for her heirs.

Trading rights were probably an important part of most of the agreements made between allied rulers and the Romans, and in most cases the tribe or state was obliged to contribute troops for the army, or more precisely, in Republican times at least, they contributed troops to fight alongside the Roman army, rather than as part of it.

The arrangements which the Romans made with client kings were theoretically tailored to the mutual needs of Rome and the particular kingdom. In Rome itself, the term *clientes* was used to describe the adherents of the upper-class senators, whose social and political standing was judged in part by the number of clients who accompanied them into the Forum or to meetings. The *clientes* rendered services to the great man, and in return received his assistance and protection. They would turn up in the mornings at the house of their patron, perhaps report on previous activities, perhaps receive money, or instructions about particular tasks, or perhaps not be noticed at all. It was a mutually satisfying way of life for both parties. Theoretically that was how it was supposed to work for the kings and allies and friends of the Roman people. The scheme had at first been applied to the Italian states and kingdoms when Rome was steadily expanding her influence over the peninsula. When the Empire began to grow, the system was used for the kingdoms bordering Roman territory. The support of the Romans often shored up the rule of the king, or sometimes queen, in his or her own lands, and help could be summoned if necessary, especially if there was an external threat that was too strong for the ruler to resist. In return for this protection, the client king was expected to furnish men, money and supplies for the Roman army whenever they were demanded, usually but not always for campaigns conducted near the king's territory.

The client kings remained attached to the Roman government of the Republic and the Empire, but until their kingdoms were annexed, as they usually were, the population was not subject to taxation as the inhabitants of the provinces were. Sometimes, however, the demands for assistance for Rome's wars could become burdensome. The security of Rome was of paramount importance to the Senate during the Republic, and to the Emperors during the Empire, so intereference in the client king's affairs was taken for granted if there was disorder in the kingdom, or external threat. On slender evidence, it is postulated that there was probably a Roman official stationed within the client king's territory to keep an eye on social and political developments. There seems to have been such an official in Thrace before Claudius annexed it as a province, but this may not have been the norm for all client kingdoms. Nothing is known of such arrangements in Britain.

Acceptance as a friend and ally of the Roman people did not exclude a Roman presence of some kind within the territory of the king, although it was not necessarily a military presence. In the Danubian lands of king Maroboduus, who actively sought an alliance with Rome, there were resident Roman traders in the first century AD, who were given the right to conduct business in the kingdom by means of the treaty of alliance, which incorporated the legal right to trade, *ius commercii*. Even before the conquest, Roman traders probably gained a foothold in southern Britain. In some of the client kingdoms Roman troops may have been sent to protect the trading communities and also the ruler, all in the interests of Rome, of course, rather than for the security of the ruler himself, in case of external attack or internal revolt which might upset the neighbouring Roman provinces. It is suggested that there may have been some Roman soldiers in Britain before the invasion under Claudius, protecting the Catuvellaunian Cunobelinus. This king is not known to have been a client of Rome, but if the suggestion that troops were present is correct, it reveals how the Romans infiltrated areas outside their provinces, and they certainly would not hesitate to do so in the case of their allies.

Since the Romans were nearly always in the ascendancy, the interests of the client kings were sometimes overruled. In Britain, after quelling some disorder, the governor Ostorius Scapula decided to disarm the Britons who had been allowed to keep their arms after the initial conquest. This order embraced the Iceni, who had voluntarily entered into alliance with Rome, and his action caused justifiable resentment. Protests were quickly suppressed, but resentment remained under the surface, re-emerging to fuel the later rebellion under Boudicca.

Client kingship was not normally hereditary, so when a king died, even if there were heirs, the kingdom was often annexed. Where there were no heirs, the kingdom was at risk from attempted usurpation, so in the best interests of the populace, the king could bequeath his kingdom to Rome, in the hope that at least there would be internal peace and protection under Roman rule. King Attalus of Pergamum took this course during the Roman Republic. Much of his wealth was siphoned off to line Rome's coffers, but this may have been a better alternative than civil war or fragmentation of the kingdom as enemies encroached upon it. For the Iceni, this arrangement did not work so well. The king Prasutagus had no male heirs, so he tried to protect the kingdom by bequeathing half of it to the Emperor, but the result was appropriation of all his wealth and lands, and gross mistreatment of his wife Boudicca and their two daughters. Then in quick succession came the subsequent revolt, total defeat, and annexation.

Other client kings in Britain were more fortunate. Togidubnus, the ruler of several *civitates* in the south of Britain, was granted Roman citizenship and seems to have enjoyed a long life under Roman protection for himself and his people. There is no evidence that the privilege of citizenship was granted to Cartimandua, but she may have received gifts of money or goods. Gifts of money and sometimes food supplies often flowed from Rome into the territory of the client king, in part to enable the ruler to maintain his position, and to reward and stabilise his warriors. Roman goods are found in the north, especially at Stanwick, which was probably fortified when Cartimandua's husband Venutius rebelled, but Roman products are even more in evidence in the territories ruled by Togidubnus. For Cartimandua, military support for her regime may have been even more important than gifts with which to control her warriors. On more than one occasion, her political struggles with her husband were sorted out by Roman troops. This is interpreted as proof of an alliance with Rome, the terms of which obliged the governors to intervene and protect the queen. If there had been no such agreement, the governors could have chosen to ignore the discord, unless Brigantian warriors erupted into the province itself. In the end, the queen herself had to be rescued and physically removed into Roman protective custody. It was not entirely unusual for client kings to end their reigns in this way. The dissidents who expelled their ruler were usually suppressed, after which the kingdom would be annexed, though in the case of the Brigantes there was a slight hiatus before this occurred.

Claudius Returns to Rome

Claudius was absent from Rome for six months, and spent only sixteen days in Britain, a lightning campaign if ever there was one. The Senate voted the title Britannicus to Claudius, awarded him a triumph, ratified all the arrangements that he had made with the tribes, and authorised the building of two triumphal arches, one in Gaul at the point of departure and one in Rome. The triumph was splendid, shows and displays were put on celebrating the conquest of the Britons, and coins celebrating Roman victories in Britain were issued in AD 46 and 49. Claudius did not jealously guard all the honours for himself, but was also quite lavish with rewards for his governors of Britain.

Before returning to Rome, Claudius disarmed the Britons, which directive probably concerned the Catuvellauni and their hangers-on, or those who had been the immediate enemy in the fighting. It was not applied universally to all tribes, since the next governor, Ostorius Scapula, made further demands for disarmament. The Claudian victory was not as complete as it was portrayed, since Caratacus had escaped, but he could not now return to the Catuvellauni, who were crushed. When Claudius left, overall command was handed back to Plautius:

> Claudius disarmed the Britons and handed them over to Plautius, authorising him to subjugate the remaining areas. (Dio 60.21)

This is the only hint as to Claudius's Imperial policy. Eventually Britain was made a province, but Tacitus says this only happened bit by bit, a process that seemed to be an ongoing development under the first two governors. After all, as Tacitus says, the Romans had merely conquered the part nearest to the Continent. This constituted, at best, a foothold rather than a province. There was still a lot to do, but it is not known how far Imperial policy intended to go, whether the Emperor Claudius considered drawing a line somewhere, retaining and administering only the parts that were profitable to the Romans, or whether he intended to conquer the whole island.

Expansion after Claudius's Visit

The ensuing campaigns in Britain while Plautius was still in command cannot be reconstructed in detail. The whereabouts of the legions can be suggested by extrapolating backwards from the points where they created their first, more permanent legionary fortresses, and sometimes it is possible to suggest their intermediate stopping points from the remains of camps, but the overall picture is considered to be much more fluid and complicated than the archaeology is able to illustrate. The legions would not move everywhere as complete bodies, but troops would be split up and used as detachments, called vexillations, or in even smaller groups, perhaps in combinations with other parts of legions or auxiliary units, to guard the previously conquered territory, to protect routes and convoys, to find and transport supplies, to build camps and temporary forts, to explore new terrain and gather intelligence. Sometimes legionaries and auxiliary soldiers would be camped together, and then moved on, perhaps in different combinations.

The most detailed information, still sparse at that, concerns the exploits of the future Emperor Vespasian. The biographer Suetonius credits him with thirty battles, the conquest of twenty towns (*oppida*) and two tribes. Unfortunately it is not stated which tribes or which towns were concerned. The one fixed point is that Vespasian conquered the Isle of Wight, specifically named by Suetonius, so it is assumed that the main areas of Vespasian's operations were in the south-west, and extrapolating from this it is conjectured that the Dumnonii and the Durotriges were the tribes that he conquered, but this is not corroborated in any of the ancient sources. The supposition is based on the geographical location of these tribes and the probable direction of Vespasian's campaign, and though it is a feasible conclusion it remains an informed guess. Vespasian's legion, II Augusta, eventually arrived at Exeter as its longer-term base, but archaeological evidence suggests that this base was not established until c.55. By then Vespasian had long since returned to Rome and been appointed to the consulship. If he was not responsible for actually placing the legion at Exeter, Vespasian perhaps moved towards the area, and his troops are probably the ones who besieged and stormed the hill fort at Maiden Castle in Dorset, and built Roman forts in the British strongholds of Hod Hill (also in Dorset) and Ham Hill in Somerset.

Before Plautius was recalled, the other legions advanced further into Britain. IX Hispana struck out northwards, leaving traces of temporary camps in its wake, but none of these sites are securely dated, and need not indicate a steady progress to its eventual fortress at Lincoln, which was founded, like Exeter, c.55. The camp at Longthorpe is the most famous of the stopping points which might belong to IX Hispana, but it is only large enough to accommodate half of the legion. Other smaller camps may have held vexillations, since the legions did not always keep together, marching as one body. Moving towards the north-west, XIV Gemina may have been camped at Leicester, and is attested at Wroxeter by a couple of undated tombstones of legionaries who had served in this legion. These tombstones may be of a relatively early date, since the legion is not listed with its Martia Victrix title, which was awarded after the rebellion of Boudicca, but the absence of such titles may simply mean that the sculptor omitted them. It does not provide definite proof of dating.

The XX legion, or part of it, was at Colchester for a few years, where its role in keeping the peace and controlling the natives would be of prime importance at this early stage in the conquest. It is not certain precisely where the fort for the XX legion was located. On the site of the British settlement at Colchester, probably on the spot where Cunobelinus had placed his own dwellings, a Roman fort has been found, but it may not be the earliest on the site. Since it is not securely dated it could just as well belong to the period after the revolt of Boudicca in 60. However, it would make an unequivocal statement to build a fort directly over the place where the king of the Catuvellauni had held court, so on balance this is perhaps the first thing the Romans built, and maybe some of the XX legion occupied it for a while.

The So-Called Temple of Claudius and the Imperial Cult

Underlining the supremacy of Rome and the Emperor, a great temple was founded in the town of Colchester. It would be a constant reminder of the conquest and subjugation of the Catuvellauni and the other tribes who were defeated with them, but whether the temple was actually dedicated to the divine Claudius during his lifetime, as is often supposed, remains unclear. Some scholars have argued that it could not have been built and dedicated to him while he still lived, because it was not customary in Rome to represent the Emperors as living gods, and in Claudius's case it would have been contrary to his stated wishes. He refused the honour when some provincials tried to dedicate places of worship to him. Others reply that in the provinces, representation of the Emperor as a living god was not frowned upon. Nevertheless, a very large Roman temple eventually appeared in the centre of Colchester, some short time after the invasion, and its podium is preserved as the foundation for William the Conqueror's equally massive castle.

It is possible that the temple was dedicated to Claudius after his death in 54, though some scholars argue that even in 60 the temple was not finished and had perhaps not been dedicated at all. However, worship of the Emperors after death, when they had become divine by means of a decree of the Senate, was perfectly acceptable to Romans in Rome and in the provinces. After Augustus was deified, it became normal practice to deify the Emperors when they died. Only a handful of Emperors were not deified, such as Nero and Domitian, who had not endeared themselves to the Senate, nor indeed to many other groups of society. Other Emperors went to their deaths in full expectation of being deified. When the Emperor Vespasian was dying, he retained his sense of humour to the very end. 'Oh dear,' he said, 'I seem to be turning into a god.'

The Imperial cult is distinct from the worship of deceased and deified Emperors. The cult was established in the provinces during the reign of Augustus. While the worship of an individual while still living was not a Roman custom, it had long been common enough in the provinces of the east, where the god-king was a well-established tradition. The Greeks were eager to render divine honours to the Roman general Quinctius Flamininus in 191 BC, after he had defeated their enemies and declared the Greeks to be free. The first Roman to be deified was Julius Caesar, in 42 BC, two years after his assassination. A convenient comet appeared in the sky at the time, which his great-nephew Octavian exploited to the full, as a sign that Caesar had indeed been taken up into the heavens and become a god. It was convenient for Octavian, as the heir of Caesar, to declare himself the son of a god, the closest he came to actual divinity in his lifetime. Caesar himself had claimed descent from the goddess Venus, but this was veiled in the mysteries of the remote past, whereas Octavian could claim a much closer relationship to a deity. When he was declared Augustus by the Senate, there were plenty of people in the Empire who were willing to worship him, but he would not allow it. As a compromise he sanctioned worship of his *genius*, or spirit, combined with worship of Rome itself in the guise of the goddess Roma. The Romans believed that people and places had a spirit, and sometimes dedicated altars to the *genius loci* or spirit of the place. From there, it was a short step to assimilating local gods, whose worship was not usually suppressed anywhere in the Roman Empire, unless it represented a threat to state security.

As a means of unification and of generating loyalty, the worship of Rome and Augustus was sanctioned throughout the Empire. In 12 BC in Lyon (Lugdunum) an altar was set up at the confluence of the rivers Rhone and Saone. The Council of the Three Gauls would meet there every year, to renew their oath of loyalty to Rome. The army also observed the cult, each individual unit swearing their loyalty in what was probably an annual ceremony.

A college of priests served the cult, called *seviri Augustales*, the majority of whom were freedmen, though the most famous example from Britain is the Roman citizen Marcus Aurelius Lunaris, who may have been a merchant, perhaps dealing in wines. He set up an altar in Boulogne in 237, declaring himself a *sevir* of the colonies of Lincoln and York. His family had probably been enfranchised in 212 when the Emperor Caracalla declared all freeborn people citizens of Rome. It was said that the Emperor's ulterior motive was to make everyone liable to pay the taxes that were levied from citizens. It may also be Caracalla who elevated the civil town at York to colonial status, since it was described as a *municipium*, or a town of lower status, when his father, the Emperor Severus, died there in 211.

The appointment as *sevir Augustalis* was an honourable one, but it was probably expensive. Tacitus says that the priests who had been chosen to officiate in the Imperial cult in Britain, just after the conquest, had to disburse large sums from their own fortunes to administer the proceedings, but in the early days there were perhaps very few of them, so the expenses would fall on only a small number of men. There was no Imperial compulsion to adopt the worship of the Emperor, so the altars that were set up in the provinces were presumably a result of local zeal, and the priests were local men who adopted the practice. The ritual centred round an altar, not necessarily accompanied by a temple building. At Lyon there was no temple. In Britain, it is likely that the altar in the courtyard of the so-called temple of Claudius in Colchester was the focal point of the Imperial cult, worshipping Rome and Augustus. By this time Augustus was a title, signifying the ruling Emperor, not the original Augustus.

The establishment of the Imperial cult in Colchester, no matter to whom the temple was dedicated, would have been particularly galling for the Britons, especially for those who had submitted voluntarily and then found out that the Roman peace actually entailed exploitation and abuse. Those men who participated in the cult would probably have been immediate targets for the rebels under Boudicca. Perhaps if the Britons had been dealt with more leniently and given time to adapt, they would have adopted Emperor-worship readily enough, but as it was, the focal point of the cult was assiduously destroyed along with the rest of the town in AD 60.

Campaigns in Wales: Ostorius Scapula AD 47 to 52

The state of play in Britain when Aulus Plautius returned to Rome to receive high honours from Claudius is not known. He probably left in the late autumn of AD 47, perhaps remaining in the province to hand over in person to Publius Ostorius Scapula, who arrived just before winter. The only source for this is Tacitus, so the chronology depends on his work, though for one short period he admits that he has conflated the events under two governors for ease of description. The first task for Ostorius was to contain the eruption of hostile tribes into the territories of those who were allied to Rome, but it is not certain which tribes were involved. The restive Britons allegedly thought that the new governor, who did not know the troops or the terrain, would probably not retaliate, especially as winter was setting in, but he did so, using the auxiliary troops, or the light-armed soldiers as Tacitus calls them.

All may have been well if the Roman action had ended there, with the identification and punishment of the ring-leaders, but Ostorius decided to pre-empt further trouble by disarming the tribes he suspected of hostility. Among them were the Iceni, who had voluntarily become allies of Rome. Finding now that Roman promises were like pie crusts, easily broken, the Iceni justifiably resented this treatment, and raised revolt, influencing their neighbours to do likewise. The Britons prepared a fortified place, surrounded by a rampart of earth, with a very narrow entrance to prevent access by the Roman cavalry. Undeterred, Ostorius attacked, ordering his cavalry to dismount and fight on foot. The subsequent defeat of the rebels quietened the other tribes, at least for the time being. Ostorius then turned his attention to Wales, attacking a tribe labelled by Tacitus as the Decangi – perhaps an error in later copies of his work, and usually taken to mean the Deceangli. Then there was some disturbance among the Brigantes of the north, which seems to have been dealt with rapidly, and peace was restored.

After this, according to Tacitus, Ostorius prepared for a campaign against the Silures of south Wales. He brought the XX legion out of Colchester, and put in its place a colony of veteran soldiers. These may have been taken from more than one legion. The Romans had planted colonies of soldier-settlers in Italy during the early Republic as a method of finding lands for time-served veterans and also employing them for the protection and control of newly won terrain, so this early colony in Roman Britain followed this pattern. According to Tacitus's timescale the colony was established in 49.

The campaign against the Silures was a difficult one. Tacitus says that a legionary base was required to keep them in order, which may mean that the XX legion from Colchester was placed in the legionary fortress at Kingsholm, near Gloucester. This site was not occupied for long. Some scholars have argued that it was founded in 48, others that it belongs to the year 49. Perhaps as early as 55 the legion moved on to the fortress at Usk, but even though it is possible to supply approximate foundation dates for the fortress sites, it is not certain which legions or parts of legions occupied them.

During Ostorius's campaign in south Wales, the Catuvellaunian king Caratacus emerged once again, as leader if not ruler of the Silures, who placed their trust in him. But he was defeated, and moved on to rally another tribe, the Ordovices in central Wales. His final battle was at a fortified site, with steep slopes on most sides. Where the ground was flatter the Britons built ramparts. There was also the added defence of a river, which may have been the Severn. In crossing this river, Scapula's soldiers suffered casualties, and while they approached the British fortifications, they were at the mercy of the missiles thrown by the Britons inside. But then they locked their shields, forming the *testudo* or tortoise with shields over their heads and at their sides, and thus protected they were able to storm the camp. Once again Caratacus was forced to run for his life, this time leaving his wife and his daughter to be captured by the Romans. He went north, to the Brigantes.

This tribe had allied with Rome on a voluntary basis, like the Iceni. By doing so, the Brigantes secured for themselves a peaceful interlude while the Romans left them alone, and though the tribal elders may have been able to foresee that this independence might one day come to an end, it was best not to provoke the Romans by harbouring a fugitive. Queen Cartimandua decided to hand over Caratacus to her allies, the Romans, an act which may be construed as treachery of the basest sort, or political common sense, depending on one's point of view. Britain was not a united country at the time, and the tribes remained very distinct from each other, concerned with their own affairs. They protected their own boundaries, and though they were usually quite ready to profit by seizing lands belonging to others, they were not always ready to throw in their lot with a disadvantaged tribe, and thereby risk the loss of what they had gained. Cartimandua was presented with a moral dilemma. There were no Romans thundering down on her borders at the moment, but if she helped Caratacus in any way, by sheltering him or giving him access to her warriors, some of whom were probably champing at the bit to go and fight the Romans, there would soon be legions not only arriving on her doorstep but breaking and entering. Caratacus may have been a brilliant and inspiring warrior leader, but his track record so far was not representative of his supposed skills. He had run away after his defeat at Colchester, and then he had joined the Silures, where he was defeated again, fled to the Ordovices, ditto, and now he wanted to rouse the Brigantes. More than likely he would bring defeat and disaster down on them too, probably while he himself fled once more to another tribe. It probably did not take Cartimandua more than a day or two to come to her decision.

Caratacus was taken prisoner and despatched to the Emperor Claudius in Rome. Tacitus devotes considerable verbiage to the spectacle of the British ruler in the capital city. He invents noble speeches for him, or perhaps in this case he adapts memories of the speeches that really were made. There is no doubt that Caratacus made an impression on the Romans. Unlike other prisoners, the

Gallic leader Vercingetorix for instance, who spent six years in prison and was then executed after appearing in Caesar's triumph, Caratacus was spared. He was allowed to live freely in Rome, in a sort of gilded cage for his retirement.

Back in Britain, Ostorius Scapula found that the Silures of south Wales were far from beaten. They used guerrilla tactics against the Romans, descending on a party of legionaries when they were building a camp, and killing the camp prefect, eight centurions and many soldiers. Then they attacked a foraging party and put up a stiff fight when Ostorius came to the rescue with some auxiliary troops. He was forced to send in his legionaries, and then the tables were turned. This battle was won but the war was destined to go on interminably. The Silures had heard that Ostorius was determined to exterminate them, and so they had nothing to lose by fighting him. Spurred on by the determination of the Silures to keep on fighting, and exasperated by the insensitive treatment meted out by the Romans, other tribes were also becoming restless. Then in 52, before he could conclude his campaigns, Ostorius died, totally worn out according to Tacitus. It is unlikely that sympathetic gestures were made by the Silures.

Trouble in the North: Aulus Didius Gallus AD 52 to 57

There was a hiatus while the province was without a governor. Claudius lost no time in choosing and sending out a fresh governor, Aulus Didius Gallus, but the time taken to deliver a message from Britain, and for the new governor to travel to the province inevitably entailed considerable delay. In the meantime, a legion commanded by Manlius Valens suffered a severe defeat. It is not known where or when this occurred. Shortly afterwards there was trouble once again in the north with the warlike elements of the Brigantes, involving an internal squabble between Cartimandua and her husband Venutius. Some auxiliary troops were sent to restore order, followed by a legion, probably the IX Hispana under its commander Caesius Nasica.

Tacitus had little or no regard for Didius Gallus, and says that the difficulties that he encountered were exaggerated, so that the victories would seem correspondingly great. He accuses Didius, who was getting on in years, of letting his subordinates do the work for him and sitting back, content to keep the Britons at arm's length. This means he made no efforts to extend Roman rule into new territories, which was always the mark of a keen general for the Romans, who thought of the Empire as without end, in both the territorial and temporal sense. Probably all that really happened under Didius was consolidation, and pacification of the tribes who had been defeated, by diplomatic means combined with demonstrations of strength where necessary. Didius had been successful as governor of Moesia on the Danube, where pacification and stabilisation were the order of the day, though he committed his troops to battle readily enough when it was necessary, and he was rewarded by Claudius. In Britain, he may have moved the legions into positions where they could keep a watch on the Welsh tribes, the XX legion to Usk, XIV Gemina to Wroxeter, and II Augusta to Gloucester. Rather than make a spectacular advance himself, he may have prepared the way for his successors.

Some scholars have seen this period as the context for the statement in Suetonius's biography of Nero that at one time the Emperor considered giving up the province of Britain. Suetonius does not supply dates or any other details, but if it is a true story, Nero may have been influenced by the fact that there was no forward movement, and it was still costing lives and precious time just to keep hold of the areas that had already been gained. The accusation against Nero may have been true, but it is worth bearing in mind that Suetonius wrote his Imperial biographies under the Emperor Hadrian, and at some point during the work, he and the Emperor seriously fell out with each other. Nero had such a bad reputation that any story told against him would probably be believed, and there was no danger of being accused of defamation of character. The wording of his accusation against Nero is perhaps significant:

> He [Nero] was never moved by any desire or hope of increasing the Empire. He even considered withdrawing from Britain, and only refrained from doing so out of deference, so that he would not appear to belittle his father's glory [meaning Claudius and the original conquest]. (Suetonius *Nero* 18)

It did not really matter if Suetonius claimed that Britain was nearly lost due to an Imperial decision some seventy years earlier, because it had patently remained Roman. What did matter, when Suetonius was writing, was what Hadrian had done. He had reversed the policy of Imperial expansion and had started to enclose the Empire within fixed boundaries. What was even more shocking was that he had deliberately given up territory that had been conquered by his glorious predecessor Trajan, known as *Optimus Princeps*, the best ruler. Trajan was technically Hadrian's 'father', just as Claudius, the conqueror of Britain, was Nero's 'father', whose glory he was unwilling to diminish. The parallel is striking. Lack of expansion always rankled with the Romans, military commanders and merchants alike, who saw potential glory and profit disappearing down the drain. Hadrian therefore, by implication, was worse than Nero. Perhaps this was merely Suetonius's scarcely veiled revenge on Hadrian, reviling him by proxy.

The Britons Become Provincials

There is very little evidence to elucidate Imperial plans for Britain. Writing nearly six decades after the conquest, Tacitus says that under the first two governors, the part of Britain nearest the Continent was made into a province. All that can be said is that the new province comprised an unknown extent of territory, and that other areas were added to it as further advances were made.

During the Republic, when a province was added to the Empire, a formal arrangement was drawn up, embodied in the *Lex Provinciae*, the law of the province. While there were certain standard requirements applicable to all provinces, this law was usually designed to encompass the individual customs and circumstances of the province and the mutual obligations of the provincials and the Romans. There is no evidence to prove whether or not this happened in Britain. The new province of Britannia, whenever and however it was formed, was an Imperial one, as opposed to a senatorial province. This distinction dates from the reign of Augustus, when he attended a meeting of the Senate, ostensibly to hand back government of the Empire to the senators, and was promptly

rewarded with numerous honours and, conveniently, the control
of the provinces containing armies. From then on, the provinces
were governed either by the Emperor via his legates, or directly by
the Senate. In certain circumstances, provinces could be reassigned,
senatorial ones being taken under the Emperor's wing, or Imperial
ones being sufficiently pacified to have troops withdrawn and to be
reallocated to the Senate.

As government of the provinces evolved, a career structure (*cursus
honorum*) for senators was established, based on Republican custom
which was adapted to meet new circumstances. Before they held any
of the important magistracies, aspiring young men of the senatorial
class usually gained experience in minor administrative offices, and
most but not all of them usually served in a legion as the senior
tribune, called *tribunus laticlavius*, or broad stripe tribune, which
distinguished them from the other five military tribunes, *tribuni
angusticlavii*, who were drawn from the equestrian class, ranking
next in line after the senatorial class. After gaining this military and
administrative experience, the next post was usually as quaestor. From
the late Republic, by decree of the Dictator Lucius Cornelius Sulla,
the office of quaestor automatically conferred entry to the Senate.
In the early Empire there were twenty quaestors, elected annually,
which provided twenty new senators each year. The quaestors were
responsible for various tasks, often dealing with finance, either in
Rome, or as financial assistant to a governor of a senatorial province.
After another five years, when they could hold further offices such as
tribune of the plebs, aspiring senators could become one of the twelve
annually appointed praetors, which opened up several further senior
posts, including command of a legion, or government of a province.
The supreme office, attainable only in a senator's more mature years,
was the consulship. There were always two consuls, elected each
year, eligible to command armies and responsible for all aspects of
government, and during the Republic they were answerable to the
Senate alone. During the Empire, consuls were recommended by the
Emperor, and in reality, though the Senate's functions were retained,
and elections were still held, the consuls were answerable to the
Emperor.

Under the Imperial system, in general, the unarmed provinces
were governed by senators who were sent out for one year, with the

title of proconsul, assisted by one of the quaestors to administer financial affairs. The governors of Imperial provinces commanded troops, but since all the Imperial provinces were technically governed by the Emperor himself, the governors acted as deputies, or legates, of the Emperor. Their titles were listed on inscriptions in abbreviated form as LEG. AUG. PR. PR., standing for the full title *legatus Augusti pro praetore*, indicated that they acted on behalf of the Emperor, as legates with praetorian rank. Although the governors of provinces with more than one legion were usually ex-consuls, who outranked the praetors, they still governed *pro praetore*. The governors of Roman Britain were usually the most senior men of their day, only equalled by the governors of Syria, the province bordering the Parthian Empire. Usually these governors had some experience of commanding troops, as *tribunus laticlavius* as young men, and then after further appointments in civilian posts, as legionary legate. They had often governed other provinces, sometimes fighting in various wars, before they arrived in Britain.

The governors of the Imperial provinces were not assisted by quaestors to look after finances. Instead a procurator was appointed, from the equestrian class, assisted by a staff of freedmen. The main tasks for the procurators of Britain were to collect taxes, and distribute pay to the troops. There was sometimes a conflict of interests in this system, since the procurator was answerable directly to the Emperor, so he could go above the governor's head, but he was presumably limited to those matters that had a bearing on finances. Not many of the procurators who served in Britain are known. The two men who were appointed before and after the rebellion of Boudicca are respectively the most infamous, and the most famous, of the handful of procurators who are attested. They were diametrically opposed in attitude, actions and reputation. The villain of the piece is Decianus Catus, whose rapacity was one of the immediate causes of the rebellion, and the hero is Julius Classicianus, who tried to make reparation for abuses that had triggered the rebellion, urging the recall of the allegedly vengeful governor, Suetonius Paullinus.

Roman society was hierarchical. Wealth was the most important attribute for any class of society, and there were rules about status. No one could become a senator without a demonstrable fortune of 1 million *sestertii*. The qualification for the middle classes of Rome, the equites or equestrians, was set at 400,000 *sestertii*. Upward mobility was not impossible, and became more common as time went on, but in all cases of advancement, aspiring equestrians and senators really needed to be noticed by the Emperor. There was tremendous snobbery among the Romans all over the Empire. When Claudius enfranchised the Gauls, making it possible for the wealthy elite groups to become senators, not many of them did so, and the attitude of the Romans to newly enfranchised provincials who became senators is epitomised by a snide remark circulated in Rome, that no one would show the new senators the way to the Senate House. Provincials did eventually penetrate into the higher ranks of Roman life, especially those from the eastern cities, where Greek culture had been established long before Romans arrived on the scene. It was the spread of Roman citizenship that enabled men from the provinces to rise high. Without it, there was no access to the senior government appointments or military commands. Many administrative posts were open to freedmen, some of whom were even wealthier than senators, but no matter how much wealth they had accumulated, in the early Empire ex-slaves could never be regarded as the equals of the equestrians or senators.

In the western provinces, where town life as the Greeks and Romans knew it had not developed, various different tribes pursued their own particular way of life, squabbled over boundaries, sometimes allying with each other and sometimes making war on each other. Their culture and religion was not necessarily primitive, and their customs were not necessarily always obliterated by the Romans, provided that the Romans could establish and maintain control. One of the customary methods of doing so in such a province was the cultivation of the local elite, in a similar fashion to the way in which the client kings were treated, but these client kings were usually situated on the borders of the province. Within the province, the most promising local rulers or families were encouraged to co-operate with the Romans. If this was successful, when the time came to devolve responsibility for local government onto the local populace, the elite groups could step in as leaders of the community.

One of the most wide-ranging and deeply felt effects of the Roman occupation would be the immediate obliteration of tribal ambitions for territorial conquest and annexation. From now onwards, that was the prerogative of the Romans. Internal strife and external boundary disputes were policed by the Romans, so any autonomy that the Britons may have hoped to retain in these respects was annihilated. They lived where the Romans said they should live, obeying new rules, and they would keep the peace with each other, or else! For most of the Britons, who were not among the favoured elite, this so-called *Pax Romana* just after the conquest did not bring peace and prosperity. The natives of a province, non-Romans, were lumped together under the heading of *peregrini*, which strictly means foreigners, somewhat galling for people living in their own land. For the first years, the Britons were under military rule as the occupation proceeded, and for many tribesmen exploitation and abuse were the only things they received from the Roman soldiers, sometimes with the connivance of the administrators.

Just as the Britons belonged to different tribes, the Romans were also ethnically diverse. The soldiers of the legions, with Roman names and citizenship, came from Italy, Gaul and Germany, and many of the auxiliary soldiers had a tribal background not unlike the Britons themselves. The administrators, and especially the traders, probably hailed from all over the Empire, perhaps speaking Greek or other languages, and using Latin for official business, and buying and selling. But however culturally diverse the occupying forces were, what united them was the concept of *Romanitas*, in which the Britons did not share. The Britons were a conquered people, and could be treated as subhuman. Tacitus records how arrogant veterans forced the British farmers off their lands, abusing them in several other ways.

It would be some time before the Romans realised that the initial treatment of the Britons was not the way to win hearts and minds; in fact it was counter-productive. The tribes who were being exploited would eventually rebel, and the tribes who were as yet unconquered would hear of the effects of Roman rule and resist more vigorously because there was nothing to lose. The way forward was to integrate, to find ways for the Romans to work with those Britons who were willing to compromise, and for the Britons to become not just allies of Rome, but to become Romans themselves. In this way, the foundations were eventually laid for the process of integration, but total Romanisation was never uniformly developed across the whole island.

The Conquest of Wales: Quintus Varanius and Suetonius Paullinus AD 57 to 60

The province was reasonably peaceful when Didius Gallus was replaced by Quintus Veranius, who had been consul in 49, and had been governor of Lycia. He started by ravaging the territory of the Silures once again, perhaps without provocation. Then he died. In his will he said that he could have conquered the province in two years. Perhaps he did not mean the whole island, but it was a boast that Tacitus, who had heard about the British campaigns of his father-in-law Agricola and his predecessors, would have found amusing.

The next governor was Suetonius Paullinus, a veteran of campaigns in the Atlas mountains in Mauretania. He was said to have been the first to cross the Atlas range, so by the time he arrived in Britain he had already earned a sound military reputation. According to Dio he was an ex-praetor when he commanded in Mauretania, so at some time after this, perhaps as a reward for his exploits, he was presumably appointed to the consulship. The date is not known, but if he was suffect consul instead of *consul ordinarius* his name would not be recorded as one of the consuls of the year. Nothing is known of his whereabouts or his appointments until he arrived in Britain, probably in 58.

Tacitus says that Suetonius had two successful years as governor of Britain, but there are no firm details as to where he operated. Wales is the most likely venue, especially as the Roman troops reached the island of Anglesey at the latter end of these two years. The fact that Suetonius Paullinus was experienced in mountain warfare, and his troops went on to campaign in north Wales, suggests that there was some element of forward planning in his appointment, as opposed to a rapid and convenient choice of any qualified candidate to replace the governor who had unexpectedly died in the middle of a campaign. It may simply be coincidence, but if the Emperor Nero had taken advice about the next most likely theatre of action in Britain, it is possible that the name of the man who had already campaigned successfully in mountainous territory would spring to mind.

It is customary to view this campaign into north Wales and Anglesey as an effort to eradicate the Druids, whose headquarters were located in the island, but it can also be regarded as a means of rounding off the conquest of Wales. To leave the island unconquered would be a threat to security, and Tacitus says that many fugitives gathered there. There were certainly Druids as well, but the campaign may not have been mounted with specific reference to them.

If Suetonius himself did not leave reports or memoirs about this episode, Tacitus was in a fortunate position as the son-in-law of Gnaeus Julius Agricola, who was *tribunus laticlavius* at this time, but the legion to which Agricola was appointed is not known. Tacitus explains that Agricola was selected to assist Suetonius on his staff, which may mean that he was attached to headquarters, but this is perhaps to read too much into the statement. The graphic description of the Britons awaiting the Romans on the shore of Anglesey may be a fanciful reconstruction on Tacitus's part, but it sounds as though it comes from personal memory, something that impressed the young Agricola.

The water separating Anglesey from the mainland was shallow, and the sands shifted with the tides, so the Roman infantry troops were ferried across the straits in flat-bottomed boats, while the cavalry waded or swam across next to their horses. The British warriors were encouraged by the Druids, earnestly praying to their gods and cursing the Romans. There were some women there as well, swathed in black clothes and waving torches. Momentarily stalled, the Romans were urged on by Suetonius, and managed to repulse the Britons. A few lines in Tacitus's account describe the savagery of their fighting. Everyone was cut down, warriors, women and Druids alike, and the religious sanctuaries among the groves of trees were torn up and burned. Then a garrison was installed; both Tacitus and Dio agree that the campaign was properly finished. It must have been a triumphant moment for Suetonius. That is, until a messenger or messengers arrived with the news that the south was in uproar. The British tribes had combined, and they were killing and burning and destroying towns, led by a woman.

3

Rebellion &
Reconstruction
AD 60 to 69

Rebellion

The rebellion of Boudicca and its suppression occupied at most several months, in reality a very short period in the history of Roman Britain, but one that has attracted a disproportionate amount of interest. It is a tale worthy of playwrights and novelists, for its epic tragic qualities, with two protagonists both fighting in desperate circumstances. The fact that one of them was a woman only intensifies the interest. It has been suggested that the role of Boudicca has been over-emphasised by the Roman authors, in order to discredit the Emperor Nero, an idea to which Tacitus may have subscribed, but which is the more readily apparent in the account written by Dio, who invents a speech for Boudicca, or Boudouika as he names her in Greek. Haranguing her troops before leading them to destroy the hated Roman towns, she reviles the Emperor, who has the title of a man but is really more like a woman, painting his face, and spending his time singing and playing the lyre. After nearly two centuries, historians such as Dio could still make good copy out of reviling Nero. This speech that Dio invents serves to present his own views, just as other ancient authors put words into the mouths of their heroes and villains, to expound the opposing points of view, and also to provide a sort of plot exposition to explain how the events had begun. The Britons would have been well aware of Nero, but it stretches credulity somewhat when, according to Dio, Boudicca compares and contrasts herself with other women, Nicotris ruler of Egypt, and Semiramis of Assyria – 'these things we learned from the Romans' she adds, as though Dio himself wished to pre-empt the question of how did a British queen know of these things.

Even if Boudicca was merely a figurehead, and the British tribes were led by some unnamed warriors, the story is too deeply embedded in the national heritage to eradicate the Queen of the Iceni as the overall commander of the rebels. She ranks with Cleopatra and Zenobia as the most powerful female enemies of Rome. Though all three of these women rulers lived at different times in very different locations, their aims were very similar, namely the preservation of their kingdoms and people. Boudicca also shares with them another feature, in that their fame obscures the fact that there is precious little information about them. At least Cleopatra and Zenobia are known by their real names, whereas Boudicca has suffered from various spellings, most famously Boadicea, which is most likely a copyist's error in the ancient sources. The more recent version of her name varies between Boudicca and Boudica – the one with the double 'c' being sanctioned by the computer spell-checker, not that this is the best authority. The version with only one 'c' is now favoured by some modern writers. The most important point is that Boudicca, however it should be spelled, may not even be the queen's real name. It may be a title, signifying Victory. In a way, she is the first Queen Victoria.

Tacitus, in the *Annals*, places the rebellion in Britain in the consulship of Caesennius Paetus and Petronius Turpilianus, the two *consules ordinarii* who gave their names to the year, which is indubitably AD 61 according to modern reckoning. Traditionally, the rebellion started in AD 60, but there is nothing apart from Tacitus's statement to throw any light on precisely when the events unfolded. The main problem is to fit everything that happened into the year 61.

Britain in AD 60-61

The rebellion seems to have taken the Romans by surprise. It probably seemed to them that the population in the areas that had been overrun were starting to settle down. Some of the local elite were adopting a Roman lifestyle, or were at least not unfriendly to the Roman government. It seemed that the military units left in the various forts, mentioned by Tacitus, could keep control while the bulk of the army went on campaign elsewhere. Three somewhat rudimentary towns had been established at Colchester, London and Verulamium. The town of Colchester was of the highest status, as a colony where veteran soldiers were settled. The status and development of London and Verulamium is not certain. Tacitus, writing towards the end of the first century, says that London was not a colony at the time of the rebellion, but he adds that it was an important centre for trade, which indicates that trading ventures were already flourishing, probably organised by Romans or Romanised provincials rather than native Britons. There would probably be a large number of culturally diverse personnel, as in any port. Although in the very early days of the conquest, the Romans administered the province from Colchester, perhaps before the rebellion of Boudicca, or a few years afterwards, London quickly became the headquarters of the governor. Since Decianus Catus fled there after the assault on the Iceni, it is assumed that London was already the procurator's administrative centre. Verulamium, which eventually became a *municipium*, or chartered town second in rank to a *colonia*, was possibly the slowest to develop, or at least archaeological investigations have revealed that although a grid pattern of streets had been established, and some shops had been built, there were few significant Roman buildings in the town at this time of the rebellion. Nonetheless it was a Roman town in spirit, most likely with Roman inhabitants and pro-Roman Britons, and it would seem to the Romans that all was set fair for peaceful development as the south and south-east started to look like a settled Roman province.

Just over fifty years earlier, the Romans had made a similar mistake. Archaeological evidence shows that in Germany in AD 9 some of the military installations were being given up for civilian development, so the newly conquered territory was poised at the point of transition between military occupation and civil administration. The governor who had been appointed was Quinctilius Varus, now almost a synonym for disaster. He had experience of Roman provincial rule in the east, where he was governor of Syria from 6 to 4 BC, and had to arbitrate between two rival contenders for the throne of Judaea, finally using armed force to quell riots. In AD 7 he was appointed governor of Germany, where he tried to hasten the formation of the province, together with the imposition of Roman law, and most importantly the levying of taxes. The Germans under their leader Arminius made it clear that they were not ready to accept Roman domination, and destroyed three legions. The Emperor Augustus used to wander about the Imperial palace shouting 'Give me back my three legions', and expansion into Germany ceased.

Both Tacitus and Dio acknowledge the abuses that had been visited on the conquered Britons. Most of the tribes may initially have been glad to be rid of the aggressive Catuvellauni, but soon found that they had jumped out of the frying pan into the fire. When the governor Ostorius Scapula put down some troublesome elements and then decided to disarm the Britons, the Iceni were the first to protest. They had allied with the Romans voluntarily and now they were being treated as the enemy. The Trinovantes too had grievances, having exchanged Catuvellaunian domination for an infinitely worse Roman version. The veterans at Colchester had been given lands to farm, which probably came from the territory confiscated from Cunobelinus's lands, but in the way of any people who feel that they are in a position to dominate and exploit, they had probably started to encroach on Trinovantian estates. Taxation had probably also begun to bite somewhat more rigorously, to the point where it was unendurable. It seems that the Romans had become too greedy, and were not supervised sufficiently well. There were many ways in which provincials could be exploited, and the Romans had centuries of practice at it. Intimidation and the extraction of protection money is not a modern invention.

How the Soldiers Supplemented Their Pay and Exploited the Provincials

As supplements to their regular pay, issued three times per year, soldiers could look forward to extra cash from a variety of sources, such as Imperial donatives, from booty, and from their own financial activities such as money lending, and property transactions, and not least little scams, protection rackets, and extortion. Augustus bequeathed certain sums to all the armed forces, including 125 *denarii* to each Praetorian Guardsman and 75 *denarii* to each legionary. Succeeding Emperors generally paid out sums to the army whenever an important victory had been won, except that Marcus Aurelius refused to do so when his finances were strained. Other Emperors paid unexpected donatives on special occasions; for example it was said that Hadrian paid a total of 70 million *denarii* to the soldiers during his reign, to mark his accession and then the adoption of his intended heir, Aelius Caesar. When his daughter married, Antoninus Pius paid out cash to the soldiers, and after the reigns of Severus and Caracalla, donatives were paid to the army more regularly.

The value of booty taken in wars is harder to assess, but it was always a possible means of increasing income. Tacitus (*Histories* 3.19.6) says that the spoils from a city taken by storm were awarded to the soldiers. Some idea of the amount of booty brought home from foreign wars can be ascertained from the monuments in the Forum in Rome, specifically the reliefs on the Arch of Titus celebrating the conquest of Judaea, and on the Arch of Severus showing the spoils from the Parthian capital.

Military men could run businesses while they were still serving, and many of them probably did so without hindrance or breaking the law, but most of the evidence for soldiers as businessmen and property owners derives from the law codes, concerning cases where there were disputes. A soldier called Cattianus serving in one of the eastern provinces sought justice because a dealer had illegally sold his slaves, and another complained that his brother had sold his share in a vineyard without asking his permission, in order to settle a debt. There is not much evidence for soldiers in business in Britain, but once the army had stopped campaigning on a regular basis and settled more permanently in forts, some enterprising men may have set up businesses, probably run by their slaves. Lending money would be one of the easiest ways to earn a profit while doing not very much except keeping an eye on the accounts and using the backing of military power to extract the repayments.

Extortion in all its forms was another means of supplementing military pay. This is securely attested in the eastern provinces, where records are better preserved than in Britain, but presumably the soldiers were no better behaved in the western provinces. The number of times that the Prefect of Egypt issued edicts to try to curb the behaviour of the soldiers only serves to illustrate that the authorities were powerless to eradicate the problem. A papyrus dating to the second century AD records the accounts of a civilian businessman who regularly entered certain sums paid to soldiers, and openly describes this process as extortion, for which he uses the Greek word *diaseismos*. This may have been a sort of protection racket, perhaps only one example among many, operated by one or two unscrupulous soldiers, or organised groups.

One of the scams outlined by Tacitus, in describing how Agricola rooted out abuses of the Britons, concerned the requisitioning of grain as part of the tax payments. The soldiers would direct the British farmers to take their grain to impossibly distant places, and then perhaps accept payments for relaxing their directives, while still accepting the grain, so the food supply was assured, the soldiers got rich, and the Britons paid twice. The serving soldiers had several methods of browbeating the natives, but once they had retired they were no better behaved. At Colchester the veterans settled in the colony forced the Britons off their lands and farmed it themselves, and probably had ways of extracting money payments or food supplies to which the military and civilian authorities turned a blind eye.

Taxation and Tribute

From ancient times it has been recognised that there are only two certainties in life, death and taxes. If government and administration is to function properly, money or goods are required to oil the wheels and pay for services, amenities and buildings. Armies require pay and supplies. The provincials were expected to make their contribution to these governmental functions, and both Strabo and Tacitus note that the Britons did not generally object to paying taxes. In addition to the provincial taxes, local taxes were levied to support the various communities. Not many self-governing towns had been established before the rebellion of Boudicca, and those that were just beginning to develop were not necessarily an expression of native ambitions, but were mostly Roman foundations, satisfying the needs of officials or traders. The *civitas* capitals, where a tribe or local community set up a central place where local government could be organised and administered, were not fully developed in the first years after the conquest. When they were established, their governing councils were made responsible for collecting both the local and the provincial taxes, supervised by the Imperial procurator and his staff, who administered the finances of the province, and were responsible for the supply and pay of the army.

There are several staple commodities that can be taxed to raise revenues: people, under the heading of the poll tax, which Boudicca complained about, according to Dio; land, based on acreage and produce; the produce itself; property; trade and commerce; and movement of goods into and out of harbours, across internal and external boundaries, and along major routes. The Romans levied taxes by all these methods. During the Republic, Roman citizens were liable for the *tributum*, an extraordinary tax that was not levied in Italy after 167 BC, when Roman coffers were beginning to swell as booty flowed in from foreign campaigns and conquests, so the acquisition of provinces paid for the running of the Empire.

Citizens were also subject to an inheritance tax of 5 per cent (*vicesima hereditarum*), levied if substantial sums were left to non-relatives. The proceeds of this tax were paid into the *aerarium militare*, the military treasury that was set up by Augustus in AD 6, in order to provide pensions for discharged veterans from the Roman army. Augustus had created the standing army from the massive numbers of soldiers still under arms in 30 BC at the end of the civil wars. Until the creation of the *aerarium militare* there was no regular scheme to pay off veterans, except for the sporadic allotment of land, which did not serve the purpose because by the time of the early Empire, soldiers were not usually accustomed to farming. Cash pension schemes were preferable by far to having lots of ex-soldiers, all superbly trained in the use of weapons, wandering over the Empire without financial support.

There were also taxes on the sale of slaves, set at 4 per cent, and on their manumission, when owners paid 5 per cent of their market value. Indirect taxes were grouped under the heading of *vectigalia*, the most important being *portoria*, the tax on goods into and out of ports and harbours and across boundaries. This tax was levied in Britain before the Claudian conquest, and the Britons were so eager to obtain Roman goods that they paid it without hesitation.

As for tax payments, they can be collected in cash or in kind. The Friesians paid in leather hides, the Britons probably in grain. All methods of collection are subject to abuses, and the Roman system did not exclude this. The most famous of the scams employed by the Romans in Britain is related by Tacitus, when Agricola tried to put an end to exploitation. When the Britons brought their grain they were ordered to take it to a collection point miles away, so they would pay to avoid the journey, or on occasion they would be forced to buy grain to meet their quotas. The quotas themselves may have been falsely measured. A bronze corn measure, dating from the reign of Domitian was found at Carvoran in Northumberland. It bears an inscription on its side stating that it holds seventeen and a half *sextarii*. It actually holds more than that. It is possible that it has nothing to do with collection of grain as payment of tax. Perhaps it was the kind of measure used by the troops when collecting their rations from the granaries inside the forts, used just like modern beer glasses where the line marking the capacity is not at the very top. But as a method of cheating the natives it would have worked wonderfully well. The British farmers were hardly in a position to protest, since it is highly likely that the military was involved in tax collection in the north of England. Instead of arguing, it would be more prudent to accept the judgement that there was not enough grain in the measure and then deliver some more, or buy it to meet the demand.

Before any tax on people and land could be levied and collected, it was necessary to assess its value, based on a survey, so when a new province was created, it was customary to take a census. Just as William the Conqueror needed to know who held which lands and what these lands were worth, the Romans needed to know the same things, how many people there were and what they produced. William waited twenty years to carry out his survey, and it did not include much beyond the River Mersey or the borders of Yorkshire. The Romans would probably not delay for an entire decade, and would not stop short of the borders of what they had overrun, since agreements with allied tribes who were not yet absorbed into the province could include the payment of tribute. The census was usually taken every five years, but not much is known about how it operated in Britain, whether a census of newly won territory would be carried out immediately every time a bit more was added, or whether the five-year cycle would apply. Only two censors are attested in the province. One was appointed to take the census of the Anavionenses in the second century. No one knows where this particular tribe lived, perhaps somewhere in north-west England, or in Scotland. In the third century, Aurelius Bassus conducted a census in Colchester.

Though the collection of taxes was supervised by the Imperial procurator, there were lower-ranking officials called *publicani* who oversaw the business at a local or regional level. During the Republic the *publicani* were notorious for corruption, and were reviled accordingly. They would bid for the privilege of collecting taxes and then set about gathering more than was supposed to be levied in order to line their own pockets. During the Republic in Julius Caesar's day, some of the *publicani* bid too much and found that they could not even meet the targets, much less get rich themselves. They had to be rescued and bailed out by the government, which has an oddly familiar sound to modern audiences of the early twenty-first century. Not much has changed in two thousand years. When the *conductores* replaced the *publicani* in the second century they were unable to resist the same temptations to feather their own nests.

For local towns of all sizes the most important revenues derived from lands, forest, mines and salt works. The money raised from these and other taxes went towards the upkeep of buildings and roads, and whatever else the local council wished to do. Councillors were also expected to embellish their towns and finance public works out of their own pockets – it was matter of honour. Sometimes local communities overreached themselves and got into trouble, either by borrowing or speculating too wildly, or by being unable to finish their grandiose projects. A local community in North Africa started to build a tunnel which went wrong, and the project had to be rescued by a military engineer. The younger Pliny encountered similar concerns when he went to govern Bithynia-Pontus; his letters to the Emperor Trajan reveal the way in which local communities could get themselves into debt or difficulties in seeing projects through. Early in the second century, investigation into such matters became more common. Town councils were theoretically autonomous, but Imperial interference was sometimes necessary when financial ignorance or incompetence threatened to result in disaster. Officials called *correctores* or *curatores rei publicae* were sent to sort out the problems.

Towards the end of the third century, taxation became more burdensome, chiefly to pay for the army. Revenues declined while expenditure rose, and external threats increased. For a while, tax was collected in kind, to supply the army, and the soldiers were paid not in cash but in rations. The Emperor Diocletian made local councillors personally responsible for the taxes, so if insufficient amounts were collected the unfortunate councillors had to make up the difference. It was not a successful scheme, resulting in great reluctance to serve in what was once an honourable position, and the wealthy classes who could afford to do so moved into the country left the towns to their fates.

The Iceni and Rome

In this climate of Roman taxation and corrupt administration, it is not surprising that Prasutagus, the ruler of the Iceni, had made provision in his will for sharing his kingdom between his family and the Roman Emperor, hoping to protect his people from the greed of the provincial officials. It is not certain how this would work, perhaps entailing outright gift of some territory so that an Imperial estate could be set up, or possibly some part of the revenues were to be earmarked for the Emperor. As an insurance policy to try to ensure that the kingdom retained at least some autonomy, it failed. Prasutagus may have died in AD 59, or perhaps early in 60, leaving his widow Boudicca and their two daughters as his co-heirs with the Emperor Nero. What happened next does not redound to Roman credit. The official in charge of financial affairs, the procurator Decianus Catus, descended on the Iceni, backed up by a few Roman troops, to claim the inheritance for Nero. He probably had another agenda as well. Now that the king of the Iceni was dead it was time to call in any loans that had been made to him by wealthy Romans, or by the Emperor. It seems that Claudius had given generous gifts to some of the British tribes, which may have been interpreted by the

Romans as loans and perhaps misunderstood by the Britons, who never envisioned having to pay it back. Rich men like Seneca were known to have lent money as well. It is possible that instructions had come from the Emperor Nero to foreclose on whatever had been lent to the Iceni, or perhaps Catus had made the decision himself. No one knows what exactly happened between the Roman procurator and the queen of the Iceni.

Boudicca Rebels

It seems that Catus and his soldiers were somewhat overzealous in carrying out his duties, whatever he thought they were, provoking an immediate protest from the Iceni. The result was that the queen was flogged, and her daughters were raped. This showed how dismally a tribe supposedly allied to Rome could be treated, in what had started out as an exercise to collect an inheritance and the associated taxes. If the procurator had not actually ordered the flogging of the queen, he clearly was not in control of his soldiers.

Catus fled, presumably returning to London, where it is thought that his administrative headquarters were located. Even if his depot was at Colchester he could hardly remain so close to the tribesmen now that this enormity had occurred. The news of what had happened would circulate among the Britons. Some of the tribes would decide that they had had enough and wanted to fight back. Others might hesitate to go to war against an army that had won all its wars up to now. Even if the Romans had been defeated in an engagement, they usually kept going and won in the end. The rallying cry for the Britons would be the mistreatment of Boudicca and what it might signify for the rest of the tribes, but behind this one event there were seventeen years of disappointment and exploitation. Normally when operating among a tribal society the Romans could rely upon internecine strife to keep the various tribes apart, making Roman domination of them so much easier. This time, some tribes sank their differences, as they had done under Cassivellaunus to oppose Caesar, and as the tribes of Scotland would do some twenty years later, under a leader called Calgacus, which may be a title, meaning the Swordsman, rather than a name.

The tribes who rose up with the Iceni will have included the

Trinovantes, and possibly other tribes of the south of the island, extending as far as south Wales. Some tribes possibly became overtly hostile without necessarily moving to join Boudicca and her army. Tacitus says that when Suetonius marched from Anglesey he did so through the midst of the enemy. It is presumed that the tribes ruled by Tiberius Claudius Togidubnus refrained from rebellion, nor did the Brigantes of the north join the rebels, though it is not known if individual warriors left their tribes in order to fight the Romans on their own account.

The chronology of the rebellion cannot be established with certainty, especially as certain events would occur simultaneously. Suetonius assembled some troops and left Anglesey as soon as he could, and marched towards the south-east, making for London, the bulk of the legionaries following after. A stream of orders will have gone out to other troops to bring them together while this march took place. There were forts in the south and south-east, perhaps manned by auxiliary troops, and the legions may have been split up, some of the soldiers having gone with Suetonius to Wales and the remainder guarding their bases. II Augusta was at Exeter in the south-west, and IX Hispana was probably at Lincoln. The legionaries from the Anglesey campaign, XIV and XX, joined Suetonius for the final battle.

In the meantime Boudicca had either already sacked Colchester or was aiming for the town. There were many veterans there but the colony had no defences for them to man, and there may have been no time to erect any barriers that might have slowed the Britons. Possibly the veterans were overconfident. They sent to Catus the procurator for help, which supports the theory that he was not in Colchester and that his headquarters lay at London. He sent 200 men, apparently not very well armed. Even if they had been armed to the teeth, the whole enterprise was useless. The Britons swept into the town, forcing the veterans and soldiers to retreat into the great temple, possibly dedicated to Claudius and possibly not even completed yet, but the building was sufficient for them to barricade themselves in. They held out for two days. The slaughter was total, including civilians.

The legate of IX Hispana, Petillius Cerialis, dashed southwards to attempt to stop the Britons, but was badly cut up and had to retreat, having lost many of his legionaries. With difficulty he managed to withdraw the cavalry and get away. It is not known whether

Cerialis had brought some mounted auxiliary soldiers with him. The legionary cavalry usually amounted to only 120 men. Cerialis retired to his camp, where he had presumably left a substantial number of men, and remained there behind his defences, according to Tacitus, who was not over-lavish with admiration for Cerialis. If it is supposed that the encounter between Cerialis's troops and the Britons took place in the environs of Colchester, or somewhere in East Anglia, the distance from Lincoln seems too great for a swift dash to the rescue, so it was once suggested that the half-size legionary camp at Longthorpe may have been the base which Cerialis came from and returned to. No one knows where IX Hispana met the Britons, who could have marched some distance north themselves. Currently it is thought more likely that the camp mentioned by Tacitus, but unfortunately not named, really was the legionary fortress at Lincoln, which had been founded *c*.AD 55.

After the disaster at Colchester the procurator Catus decamped once again, this time out of harm's way to Gaul, leaving Britain to its fate. Tacitus puts the blame for causing the rebellion firmly on Catus's shoulders. The procurator's rapacity was not the only grievance that the Britons suffered, but if he had not descended on the Iceni and the terrible events there had not occurred, it is possible that an outright rebellion could have been avoided, while resentment simmered but did not boil over.

Suetonius Abandons London

Suetonius finally arrived at London and decided that he could not defend the town. He gave the order to abandon the area, allowing anyone who could keep up with the army to accompany him. It was the correct decision from the military point of view, since there were no defences surrounding the town, and even if there had been a bank and ditch or a palisade, his army would have been worse than useless if he allowed it to be surrounded and possibly trapped in defence of only one town. It would be better to meet the Britons in the open, when he could expect to have more men. The legionaries and auxiliaries that he had summoned ought to have been on the march to join him by now. On his way out from London he brought the troops from the forts in the immediate area, and he was finally joined by the XIV and XX legions. He had about 10,000 men, and would have had more if only II Augusta had marched, but its commander, the camp prefect Poenius Postumus, refused to move. Various suggestions have been made to explain why he did not lead his troops out. He was only third in command, apparently without the legionary legate or the senior tribune, who had perhaps accompanied Suetonius to Anglesey with a detachment. Postumus may have been overcautious in the absence of more senior officers. He may have commanded a reduced garrison, and there may have been restless tribes all around him who made it dangerous for him to leave his post. But no one really knows why he did not march.

London was quickly overrun by the Britons. All remaining inhabitants were killed, and the buildings put to the torch. Excavations in London around the Cornhill area have turned up burnt layers nearly one foot thick, so this may be where the main concentration of buildings lay and where the Britons concentrated their attack. Next it was the turn of Verulamium, where there was a defensive bank of earth and a surrounding ditch but seemingly no one to man the defences. Tacitus says that the Britons avoided the hard work of attacking forts and went for the places where there was no defending force, and rich booty was to be found. About 70,000 people were killed, according to Tacitus, whose description of atrocities is quite restrained, limited to hanging, burning and crucifying. He perhaps knew more, since his father-in-law Agricola was there as a young man, in his post as *tribunus laticlavius*, the senior tribune of a legion, and perhaps with Suetonius's army at the time. It is Dio who provides the lurid details. He describes women with their breasts cut off and stitched into their mouths, and people impaled on stakes. His source material is not known. There may have been official records, or he may have drawn on folk memory. It may all be true. By the twenty-first century no one should be surprised at what human beings, especially those with a grudge, are capable of doing to other human beings.

The Battle

With fewer men than he had hoped for, Suetonius chose his own battleground to meet the Britons. It is not known where this was, but is generally agreed to be somewhere in the Midlands, possibly at Mancetter where a case has been made for it by comparing the geography of the area with what Tacitus says about the battle site. Suetonius placed his troops with a wood at their backs, facing an open plain which afforded no opportunity for the enemy to mount an ambush. The approach to this site was narrow, which would force the Britons to bunch up. The formation of the battle line was classic. The legionaries were placed in the centre, flanked by the light-armed auxiliary troops, with the cavalry units on both wings, called *alae*, the traditional place for the mounted units, which were called *alae* themselves. The British warriors were accompanied by their families, who drew up behind them in their carts and wagons, like many other tribal war bands.

This is where Tacitus invents speeches for Boudicca and Suetonius to set the scene. Rather than trying to quote her words in direct speech, Tacitus summarises what the queen was supposed to have said, using reported speech to paint a picture of Boudicca and her two daughters riding around in her chariot to harangue each of the tribes. She reminded them of what had occurred at the hands of the Romans, and what might happen if there was no resistance. She said that a legion had been destroyed, which refers to Cerialis and IX Hispana. She pointed out that some of the Romans were hiding in camps, while the rest would not be able to withstand the numbers of warriors that she had brought to this battle. The numbers of tribesmen that were mustered were probably formidable. Tacitus gives the vague description *quanta non alias multitudo*, numbers not seen before, but Dio's estimate of 230,000 warriors at the final battle sounds dubious.

Suetonius's speech, in Tacitus's version, was short. The general pointed out that enemy was numerous but not well armed and they would not stand up to soldiers who had always been victorious. He urged the men to keep close together, and after they had thrown their javelins, to fell the Britons with their shields and swords, without stopping to gather booty. Then he gave the signal for battle.

Dio really goes to town with his speeches, presenting two opposing points of view, in direct speech, almost a theatre piece which would sound so much better when his account was read out loud to an audience. Putting words into Boudicca's mouth, he emphasises the enslavement of the Britons and the injustices heaped upon them. He describes the weakness of the Romans as opposed to the way the Britons live. Whereas the Romans need shelter and defences, and they expire if they cannot have their bread, wine and oil, the Britons are tougher, living on whatever they can find. Since this was written in the third century, Dio probably resorted to rhetorical platitudes about the barbarians, as the Romans called most people who were not Roman. He also includes an anecdote, whereby Boudicca, in order to divine the future, released a wild hare from her tunic, which ran away into the area that the Britons considered lucky. This omen gave great encouragement to the tribesmen. For Suetonius's speech, Dio imagines the governor going the rounds of each division of the army, encouraging them to show how superior they were to the natives, and emphasising the need for revenge, and ending with the 'conquer or die' theme.

The reality was no doubt quite different. The legionaries threw their javelins and then charged in wedge formation, cutting through the British tribesmen, and the auxiliaries and the cavalry using their lances. When the Britons tried to flee they were hampered by the wagons behind them, and about 80,000 of them – according to Tacitus – were killed, for a cost of 400 Roman dead. No one knows what happened to Boudicca and her daughters. She may have been killed in battle, or as Dio says, she may have fallen ill and died a short time later.

Aftermath

The war was over except for the mopping up, but this was a momentous task, with three towns that had been developing along Romans lines utterly destroyed, and an immediate need for replacement troops. Tacitus says that 2,000 infantry, 8 auxiliary cohorts and 1,000 cavalry were despatched from Germany. It seems that the greatest losses had been sustained by IX Hispana, since Tacitus immediately adds, after giving the totals, that this legion was brought up to strength. He may not have been exaggerating, presumably having obtained these figures from his father-in-law Agricola, or even from some reports of Suetonius Paullinus himself.

The story that Nero once considered abandoning Britain, as reported by the biographer Suetonius Tranquillus, has already been mentioned in the previous chapter, but if it is true, then surely it belongs to this episode, when the losses were totalled up and reported back to Rome. If the auxiliary cohorts are reckoned in round figures at about 500 men in each, then the total numbers of replacements that were required in order to bring the British garrison back to functional strength exceeds one complete legion. Tribesmen were not supposed to have the organisational skills or the capability of wiping out Roman troops, so it was a double disaster: a severe loss of manpower, and a blow to Roman pride. Even if this did not lead to thoughts of abandonment, the news would have been very disturbing in Rome. Nero would lose face, and at this moment he still had some face to lose, since he had not yet become the monster that he turned into later. But a quick talk by the statesman Seneca and others may have dispelled any such ideas of abandonment from the young Emperor's mind. Most likely it was pointed out to him that there would be a considerable loss of revenues if Britain were to be evacuated.

The condition of the Britons was desperate. Suetonius placed his cohorts and cavalry in new winter quarters, and sent them out to harass the tribesmen, and as Ostorius Scapula had done some years before, Suetonius probably included tribes merely considered dangerous as well as those who had joined the rebellion. There was no food, because the Britons had relied on the capture of Roman supplies, and had not bothered to plant crops before they set out. It is unlikely that Suetonius and his soldiers cared about any of the Britons, even those who had kept the peace. Revenge as well as mopping up resistance seemed to have been the order of the day. Suetonius and the soldiers had seen for themselves what the rebels had done.

The new procurator, on the other hand, had not. Julius Classicianus, who was sent to Britain to replace the disgraced Catus, was a Gallic noble with Roman citizenship, and was sympathetic to the plight of the Britons. He probably saw more clearly than the governor Suetonius that harsh treatment of the natives, who were resentful and now hungry, could only be detrimental. Retribution is never designed to win hearts and minds, and in Roman Britain it would interfere with government, administration, the production of grain, the promotion of trade, and the collection of taxes, the latter being Classicianus's main responsibility. From the beginning, he and Suetonius seem to have clashed, and Classicianus allegedly told the Britons who complained to wait for the appointment of a new governor. He perhaps sent reports to Rome to reiterate this, recommending that Suetonius should be recalled.

Something of the sort prompted Nero to send his freedman secretary Polyclitus to Britain to try to reconcile the governor and the procurator, and no doubt he was ordered to bring back a report on the state of affairs in the island. Trailing an enormous entourage through Gaul, Polyclitus arrived and assessed the situation, to the astonishment of the Britons, who did not understand how or why an ex-slave should be able to wield such power. The report to Nero was possibly reassuring, or if the true situation was revealed it was decided to allow Suetonius to remain as governor for the time being. Then he apparently lost some ships and their crews, which is usually described as a valid reason to recall him, but one wonders whether Nero, who was able to give orders to the great general Domitius Corbulo to fall on his sword, needed any valid reason to replace a governor. Nero and his advisers were probably waiting for a suitable opportunity, in order to save Roman sensibilities, seizing upon the loss of ships as the official excuse to have Suetonius recalled. It would not be advisable to give the Britons the satisfaction of seeing the governor removed solely because of his harsh treatment of them.

A Change of Policy

The new governor Petronius Turpilianus was consul in 61, and as his office came to an end, perhaps after only a few months, he set out for Britain. Tacitus says that he was lenient, and willing to listen to the Britons. The activities of the two years that he spent in Britain are virtually unknown. The rebuilding of the shattered towns was no doubt the most important of his priorities, but there are only vague hints of what he may have achieved, for instance the first phase of the Forum in London may have been started under Turpilianus. There was no military activity to speak of, not unusual in the circumstances perhaps, but Tacitus, ever the advocate of expansionism, accuses

Turpilianus of idleness. It was a peaceful province that was handed over to Marcus Trebellius Maximus in 63. Some of the credit for promoting the peace must go to Classicianus, whose work after the removal of Suetonius is not recorded. He probably worked closely with Turpilianus and then Trebellius, but he died in office, perhaps *c*.63 or 64. His wife set up a funerary monument for him in London, which can still be seen in the British Museum.

The origins and background of Trebellius Maximus are obscure. His term of office in Britain was a long one, but although it began well, it ended badly when the civil war erupted after the death of Nero. There was no military action under the new governor, and in the absence of forward campaigns, four legions were somewhat superfluous. In 66 or 67, one of them, XIV, now with the title Martia Victrix for its part in the defeat of Boudicca, was withdrawn by Nero, along with eight auxiliary cohorts of Batavians. They were destined for a campaign in the Caucasus. For a short time the legionary complement of Britain comprised II Augusta, IX Hispana, and XX Valeria Victrix, the title bestowed on it for its part in suppressing Boudicca.

Trebellius may have been responsible for moving the XX legion out of Usk to resettle in Gloucester, a somewhat retrograde movement since it had moved from Kingsholm near Gloucester only a few years before. Alternatively, some scholars think that it may have gone to Wroxeter when XIV was recalled by Nero, but for XX that move probably occurred some years later. II Augusta and IX Hispana remained respectively at Exeter and Lincoln. The soldiers were no doubt kept busy on patrols, carrying out police work, securing supplies, perhaps even helping to rebuild the towns, but they were not given the opportunity for military action. Inactivity for prolonged periods was not good for army morale, and boredom and discontent set in. The XX legion perhaps had more cause for complaint than the others, because it had been moved around much more frequently from one base to another. The legionary legate, Roscius Coelius, took it upon himself to be the spokesman for his own XX and the other legions, and rapidly became the leader of the restless troops. He accused Trebellius of impoverishing the legions, which might mean that pay was in arrears and Trebellius had done nothing to remedy the situation, but it could also imply that without profitable campaigns, the soldiers were deprived of a means to collect booty and get rich quick. Trebellius may also have tried to put a stop to the various schemes that soldiers could set up to exploit the natives, given that he had possibly been ordered to placate the population and keep the peace so recently won.

Hard Times

The period after the rebellion of Boudicca is a dark age, singularly devoid of sources, either literary or epigraphic, and as far as can be discerned from archaeology, recovery in the devastated towns and countryside ranged from slow to non-existent. It was probably just as much a period of stasis in the civilian and administrative spheres as it was in military circles, so perhaps the reason why it is not possible to elucidate what was happening is because not much was actually happening. After the rebellion was crushed, the people of Britain were in dire straits, probably for some considerable time. In the year after the rebellion, many farms presumably still stood empty in the lands of the Iceni and Trinovantes. Even if the numbers of tribesmen killed in the battles are exaggerated in the ancient sources, there would be very many who never returned to their lands. Some of those who did return may have been rooted out and executed, or sold as slaves while Suetonius exacted his revenge. Defeated tribesmen would probably be declared *dediticii*, a title reserved for people who had surrendered, and were deprived of all rights. If this was the case, then some of them may have been recruited into the Roman army and sent away from the province. It was usual practice to remove potential troublemakers in this way, especially after the conclusion of a war. During the civil war of 69, Tacitus says that the Roman general Caecina commanded a motley collection of Gauls, Lusitanians and Britons. The status of these Britons is unknown. They may have been volunteers, but they could just as easily have been defeated tribesmen removed from their homes after the rebellion of Boudicca.

The Iceni were not exterminated, as demonstrated by the later foundation of their capital at Caistor-by-Norwich, named Venta Icenorum for the tribe. But it is significant that it was not properly established until the reign of Hadrian, and remained smaller than other tribal capitals. Despite its location in a fertile area, near enough to the coast, Caistor-by-Norwich did not develop as did, for instance, the capital of the Dobunni at Cirencester (Corinium Dobunnorum), which flourished and became the second largest town in Roman Britain.

The possible scenario of the later AD 60s is demonstrated by the archaeological excavation of one Roman villa, at Gorhambury, near Verulamium. It had started out probably as a British farm, or a collection of a few huts, but just before AD 60 a Roman-style villa was built. Then after the rebellion the inhabitants on the site, either the existing ones or new farmers, reverted to living in huts. Sometime later, the residents tried again, and a new villa was built. Verulamium itself did not recover rapidly after the destruction and burning, as though there was no one to invest in new buildings, or the momentum had run down.

One place where reconstruction seems to have begun quite soon after the rebellion is London. If it was the administrative headquarters of the procurator and probably also the governor by this time, the impetus for recovery most likely came from the Imperial administration. A new Forum was laid out at this time. It would be another decade before the structure identified as the governor's palace was planned and built, though this need not mean that the governor himself and his administrative staff were located in some other town. Since London was also an important trading centre, the merchants and traders would have a vested interest in setting the town on its feet once again. They were in a better position than the native Britons to make profits, so they may even have contributed the money to kick-start the proceedings. Usually town building was funded by the local community, but in this case the government may have helped, and the army may have done some of the building work, though this is not proven. Building materials were used bearing government stamps, but it is not known if the inhabitants of London paid for them.

The Civil War in Rome

In AD 69, when British civic and commercial life may have been reviving, the Roman world lurched into a home-made crisis, and everything was put on hold. There was hardly anyone left who had a good word for Nero, but the unifying influence of opposition failed to produce any consensus of what to do about the situation. The Roman world was divided into factions who were prepared to fight each other. In 68, the governor of Gallia Lugdunensis, Julius Vindex, sounded out other governors to try to persuade them to join him in a revolt against Nero, who had lost the support of every class of society. Eventually he was forced to commit suicide in June 68, allegedly proclaiming 'What an artist dies in me!' The legions of Upper Germany suppressed Vindex, but then tried to appoint their governor Verginius Rufus as Emperor. He refused politely, which was a courageous act in the presence of thousands of men armed with swords. In Spain, the troops promoted their own governor, Galba, as the next Emperor. He marched to Rome where he received the support of the Praetorian Guard and became Nero's successor. But then after seven months the Praetorians changed their minds, killed Galba, and chose Otho in his place, in January 69.

Only a few days before the elevation of Otho, the troops in Germany proclaimed Vitellius, so there were now two Emperors. The three legions in Britain supported Vitellius, who summoned a total of 8,000 men from the British garrison to join him. It may have been at this moment that the governor Trebellius Maximus was forced to leave Britain by the machinations of Roscius Coelius, legate of XX Valeria Victrix. Trebellius supported Vitellius and perhaps went with the 8,000 legionaries to join him.

While two rival claimants for the Empire fought it out, chaos reigned in Gaul and Italy. There was no official governor in Britain, except the self-appointed Roscius who took charge of affairs for a short time. It is significant that the legions did not rush headlong to Vitellius even though they sided with him, and neither did the Britons of the south take advantage of the situation to rebel once more. They may have been too thoroughly suppressed to try, but they may also have begun to settle down, beguiled by the trappings of Roman civilisation, which Tacitus sneers at, saying that it marked their enslavement. Some of them had become accustomed to a life of leisure and luxury, Roman style.

The Vitellian troops defeated Otho in April 69, so Vitellius was now sole Emperor. He appointed a governor to Britain, Marcus

Vettius Bolanus, who had been consul in 66. Vitellius decided to remove XIV legion from Italy, where the soldiers were becoming unruly. He ordered it to march back to Britain. They set fire to a part of Turin as they were leaving. The legion and the governor may have arrived in Britain together, and XIV may have gone to Wroxeter, only to be withdrawn and stationed on the Rhine a short time later. Tacitus dismisses the new governor Bolanus as ineffective, because he was unable or unwilling to impose discipline on the fractious troops.

When the Brigantes started to fight among themselves, Bolanus had to intervene and restore order. It was the usual story of a ruler being ejected and appealing to Rome for assistance. In this case it was Queen Cartimandua who had fallen out once again with her husband Venutius, who had already caused similar trouble for the governor Didus Gallus. The queen had divorced Venutius and married his armour bearer Vellocatus, so her ex-husband and the anti-Roman groups retaliated and fought against the queen. Venutius was no doubt fully aware of the power struggles going on in Rome, and of the surly mood of the legionaries in the south of Britain, so he probably reckoned that there would never be a better chance to seize power. The unrest among the legions may be the reason why Bolanus sent some auxiliary units northwards to Brigantia, without legionary back-up. There were some skirmishes, perhaps, but in the end the Romans had no choice but to extricate Cartimandua and leave Venutius in power. Then, as Tacitus says, the kingdom was left to Venutius and the Romans were left with the war. But it was not fought for another year or two, under a different governor. It is easy to blame the governor Bolanus for his apparent lack of enterprise in not marching in to gain control of the territory and pursue Venutius, but it was a very large area, with mountainous terrain that the Britons knew well. Apart from the fact that the Roman troops may not have been reliable, such a campaign in the north needed more detailed planning and the assembly of battle groups and of supplies, for which Bolanus may not have been ready. He may have considered that the southern parts of Britain, especially south Wales, were not sufficiently pacified for troops to be withdrawn for a campaign in the north. On the other hand, a poem by Statius addressed to Bolanus's son suggests more than just passive acceptance of the status quo in the north, referring to the building of forts, and in a cryptic remark he suggests that Bolanus won a breastplate from an unnamed British king, so there may have been more military action than is discernible in the pages of Tacitus.

The forts referred to in Statius's poem may have been built to contain the Brigantes without encroaching on their territory. There were already a few forts on the southern border of Brigantia, a small one at Templeborough and larger forts at Rossington Bridge, Broxtowe and Osmanthorpe, which had been established by previous governors, either by Ostorius Scapula or perhaps Didius Gallus, who had been obliged to assist Cartimandua some years earlier. It has been suggested that Bolanus placed forts in the territory of the Parisi, a tribe living to the east of the Brigantes, particularly at Malton, where a large fort was built, capable of housing part of a legion, or more than one auxiliary unit. It remained in occupation even after the legionary fortress of York was built. At best, from the archaeological evidence, it can be said that Bolanus contained the situation, but was unable to embark on full conquest of the north, while the whole Roman world held its breath, waiting to find out who would finally emerge as Emperor.

In Rome Vitellius tried to unite the shattered Roman world by sparing the men who had opposed him, and issuing coins proclaiming the unity of the army. But in the eastern provinces, two men were watching and waiting. Titus Flavius Vespasianus had been appointed governor of Judaea, in the latter half of 66, to quell the revolt that had broken out there. It was said that Vespasian had committed the unforgiveable error of dozing off, probably bored out of his mind, while Nero was reciting poems on his literary tour of Greece. The Judaean appointment was Vespasian's reward for this transgression. At about the same time, Vespasian's colleague Gaius Licinius Mucianus was appointed governor of Syria. They had been corresponding for some time, through the medium of Vespasian's son Titus. When they heard that Galba had been proclaimed Emperor, Titus set off to congratulate him, but he had travelled only as far as Corinth in January 69, when he heard that the Praetorians had killed Galba and proclaimed Otho, and at about the same time, the Rhine legions proclaimed Vitellius. Titus turned back. If Vespasian and Mucianus had not already discussed the possibility of making a bid for the Empire, they probably started now. Tacitus says that the instigation came from Titus, but it was Vespasian who was spontaneously proclaimed Emperor by the two legions in Egypt on 1 July 69, followed by his own troops in Judaea two days later, and then by Mucianus's soldiers shortly afterwards. The alleged spontaneity had probably taken several months to organise. The rallying cry was then, and forever afterwards, the illegitimate rule of Vitellius and the chaos he had brought to Italy. Vespasian was to be the saviour of the state, not just an adventurer who fancied a taste of supreme power. The Jewish historian Josephus and the immediate court circle faithfully propagated the image. Vespasian himself did not march on Rome immediately, remaining in Judaea until he could safely hand over the command to his son Titus. In Vespasian's place, Mucianus set off overland to Italy in August 69, and fortunately the Flavians had an ally in Antonius Primus who was in Pannonia and therefore much closer to Italy. He was the commander who faced the Vitellian troops at the battle of Cremona and won. He had done more than anyone to win the Empire for the Flavians, but his big mistake was to allow his soldiers to sack Cremona, a blot on Vespasian's rule that had to be eradicated, so Primus was sacrificed. It was given out that he had disobeyed Vespasian's orders, so the new regime could distance itself from the carnage.

In Britain, a new era was about to start. Gnaeus Julius Agricola was appointed legionary legate of XX Valeria Victrix in 70, replacing the troublesome Roscius Coelius. The governor Vettius Bolanus was left in post until 71, when he too was replaced by Petillius Cerialis. After some years of stasis, the advance was to begin again.

4

Almost the Whole Island AD 69 to 96

Flavian Expansion

The term 'Flavian' derives from the family name of the three Emperors who reigned from AD 69 to 96: Titus Flavius Vespasianus, who was proclaimed in 69, and his two sons who became successively the Emperors Titus (79 to 81) and Domitian (81 to 96). In Britain throughout this period there were major advances in both the military and civilian spheres. The three known governors who were appointed by the Flavians conquered the rest of the island, and during their tenure of office there were considerable developments in the towns and cities, perhaps encouraged by the governors whenever the natives expressed an interest in adopting Roman forms and fashions. The process of Romanisation was once construed as an active policy on the part of the Emperors, carried out through their governors and the Roman armies, but now it is seen as a piecemeal development more dependent on example and native initiative than on Roman prompting.

The three known Flavian governors are Petillius Cerialis, Julius Frontinus and Julius Agricola. From about 84 there is little information about the governors of Britain, until c. 118. Compared to the brief notices that have survived about the first two, Cerialis and Frontinus, there is a disproportionate amount of information about the third, Julius Agricola, because the historian Tacitus married Agricola's daughter, and wrote a biography of his father-in-law. The major problem is to match the archaeological information with what the sources tell us about the activities of these governors, particularly those of Agricola, seemingly so well described but with a frustrating lack of identifiable place names.

Conquest of the Brigantes: Petillius Cerialis AD 71 to 73/74

Quintus Petillius Cerialis Caesius Rufus was the legate of IX Hispana at the time of the revolt of Boudicca. Unfortunately he did nothing to enhance his reputation by dashing to the rescue and being soundly beaten by the Britons, but later he chose to take the side of the Flavians apparently from the very beginning. It has been suggested that after the rebellion of Boudicca was crushed, the troops sent as replacements from Germany were accompanied by Vespasian's son Titus, who was a military tribune in Britain at some unspecified time. It seems that the majority of the legionary soldiers were needed to fill the ranks of IX Hispana, so it is just possible that Cerialis met Titus at this time. At any rate Cerialis joined the Flavians in December 69, before Vespasian arrived in Rome, and he appears to have married Vespasian's daughter, Flavia, perhaps as his second wife.

As a trusted member of Vespasian's circle, in 70 Cerialis was chosen, with Annius Gallus, to suppress the revolt of Civilis and the Batavians on the Rhine. This rebellion had been prompted by Antonius Primus, the general who defeated the Vitellian troops at Cremona. He incited the revolt as a short-term means of keeping the Vitellian troops of Germany too busy to intervene in Rome, but the rebellion had spiralled out of control, and it required an army to put it down. To assist in this endeavour, XIV legion was brought back from Britain. The legionaries had probably not yet had time to unpack properly since Vitellius returned them to Britain because they were causing trouble in Italy. This was the final removal; the legion never returned to Britain. Cerialis may have been rewarded with the consulship for his exploits in suppressing the rebellion. According to the Jewish historian Flavius Josephus, who had joined Vespasian in Judaea, Cerialis was consul in 70, most likely as suffect consul, since his name is not quoted as one of the eponymous consuls of that year.

His next appointment was as governor of Britain, in 71. There had been little or no advance in the province since the rebellion of Boudicca, though there had been some trouble with the Brigantes which the previous governor Bolanus had merely contained, since it was not the most auspicious time to embark on a northern campaign. The situation that Cerialis inherited was somewhat threatening, since the Brigantes were no longer ruled by the pro-Roman Queen Cartimandua. Her husband Venutius had been left in charge when the queen was rescued, and there was probably no shortage of anti-Roman warriors who would rally around Venutius if he decided to go to war.

There were a few early Roman forts, built of turf and timber, on the edge of Brigantian territory, at Templeborough and Rossington Bridge, Broxtowe and Osmanthorpe. These forts may have been in existence since the days of Didius Gallus, or even earlier. Bolanus may have built the large fort at Malton in the lands of the more peaceful Parisi, to guard the east flank of the Brigantes. There are probably more turf and timber forts awaiting discovery. The known forts on the southern borders and flank of Brigantia would hardly be enough for control of the whole territory, which covered most of northern Britain, up to the River Tyne and the Solway. With Cerialis's arrival, Roman policy changed from one of containment to active invasion. There were now only three legions in Britain, and only a short time earlier Vitellius had taken a contingent of 8,000 men from the province to shore up his army in his bid for power. In manpower terms this approximates to one and a half legions. To make up the numbers Cerialis brought with him II Adiutrix from Germany. It may have gone to the fortress at Lincoln, which was occupied by troops until *c*.77 or 78, while IX Hispana, Cerialis's old legion, probably went to York, where the fortress was founded *c*.71. Very little of the speculation about which legions were based in which fortresses is proven by incontrovertible evidence, so these suppositions may one day be overturned if new evidence comes to light. Troop dispositions were in any case quite fluid as the wars were fought, and vexillations and sometimes whole units moved from place to place in quick succession, splitting up and recombining as they progressed through the country.

In describing Cerialis's former exploits, Tacitus has little respect for him, insisting that in the suppression of the Batavian revolt Cerialis's success was due to good luck rather than good management. In Britain, the general is represented in a more favourable light:

> Petillius Cerialis at once struck the Britons with terror by attacking the state [*civitas*] of the Brigantes, said to be the most populous in the province, and in many battles, some of them bloody, he conquered a great part of Brigantia ... Indeed Cerialis would have overshadowed the exploits and reputation of any other governor, but Julius Frontinus, a great man, sustained the burden. (Tacitus *Agricola* 17)

The troops that Cerialis took with him on campaign are not known. Out of loyalty to IX Hispana he probably gave this legion the chief role in the campaign, advancing into the eastern parts of Brigantia, and it has been suggested that he allowed the legate of XX Valeria Victrix, Gnaeus Julius Agricola, to command in the west, to effect a pincer movement on the tribesmen. Agricola was certainly given independent commands, according to Tacitus:

> At the beginning Cerialis only shared with Agricola the hard work and the danger, but eventually he shared the glory as well. Frequently he tested him with command of part of the army, and sometimes, judging by results, he gave him control of larger forces. (Tacitus *Agricola* 8)

It is suggested that Cerialis reached Carlisle, and probably penetrated into southern Scotland. The first known fort at Carlisle has yielded early Flavian pottery and coins, and the timbers of a gateway were shown by dendrochronological analysis to have been felled in 72 or 73. In the east it is not clear where the Romans campaigned, but perhaps they arrived at the Tyne as well as the Solway. Somehow the fort at Castleford in Yorkshire and the half-legion base at Malton have to be fitted into the picture, and it is not certain how much was achieved by Bolanus when he contained the Brigantian revolt. Marching camps over the Stainmore pass across the Pennines, and a series of camps around Carlisle, have been attributed to Cerialis, as part of his pursuit of the Brigantian king Venutius. Temporary camps are notoriously difficult to date, and a line of marching camps gives no information about which troops were using them, or in which direction they were marching. Nonetheless it seems that Tacitus was correct to say that Cerialis had overrun nearly all of the territory of the Brigantes. Unfortunately he does not outline the next stage, of garrisoning the area and dealing with the natives.

Conquest of the Silures: Julius Frontinius AD 73/74 to c. 77

Sextus Julius Frontinus is better known as an author than as a governor of Britain. He was placed in charge of the aqueducts and water supply of Rome, and wrote a manual on the subject, called *De aquae ductu urbis Romae*. He may have accompanied the Emperor Domitian to Germany in his campaigns against the Chatti, or at least he prudently mentioned a few of Domitian's activities in his book called *Strategemata* on military stratagems. Frontinus is a sterling example of the versatility of Roman high officials; he commanded armies, governed provinces, investigated engineering, improved the water supply, studied military history and wrote books. He will certainly have had experience of civil administration as well, but not much is known about his career, except that in 70 he was urban praetor in Rome. This was an important post, in which he would act as chief magistrate when the consuls were absent. He may have commanded an army group formed from vexillations in the suppression of the revolt of Civilis. Before he was appointed governor of Britain he must have been consul, but it is not known in which year.

The only information that has come down to us about Frontinus's term of office in Britain derives from Tacitus, namely a bald statement that the new governor conquered the Silures of south Wales. This leaves open to interpretation what else he may have achieved. Some scholars argue that he did nothing in the north of Britain, while others suggest that he could not have left the whole area unattended. There may have been unrecorded Roman activity under the direction of one of Frontinus's officers, even if this activity entailed merely consolidation of what Cerialis had achieved. Frontinus probably operated in north Wales as well as the south. He is credited with the foundation of the legionary fortress at Chester, which was still being built when Agricola took over, and besides the legionary base it is highly likely that Frontinus established some auxiliary forts in north Wales. A cavalry unit stationed in Ordivician territory was badly cut up just before Agricola arrived, and it is probably safe to assume that this unit was not there in complete isolation.

The campaign against the Silures was hard fought, but ultimately successful. It may have been Frontinus who founded the *civitas* capital of the Silures at Caerwent (Venta Silurum). If this seems a little too precipitate, coming directly after the war, there is a parallel from the German provinces, when Gnaeus Domitius Corbulo campaigned against the Friesians, or Frisii, in the reign of Claudius. This tribe had hitherto been quite loyal to the Romans, but had erupted in protest when their taxes were increased. They did not pay in cash, but in hides, and all went well until a somewhat insensitive Roman official decided to increase the standard size of the hides to that of the aurochs, a truly enormous beast which has been extinct since the seventeenth century. It was too huge and powerful for the Frisii to rear on farms or to capture and skin on a regular basis, and their own beasts did not even begin to approach it in size. The result of this impossible request was a rebellion, which Corbulo suppressed, and then according to Tacitus, the defeated Friesians gave hostages, and settled in the area that he marked out for them, imposing on them a senate, magistracies and laws.

Conquest of the North: Gnaeus Julius Agricola AD 77/78 to 83/84 & the First to the Third Campaigning Seasons AD 77 to 70

The conquest of the Silures, the foundation of the legionary fortress of Chester, and perhaps the establishment of the *civitas* capital at Caerwent is the sum total of what is known or broadly surmised about the governorship of Sextus Julius Frontinus, unlike his successor Gnaeus Julius Agricola whose biography by his son-in-law Tacitus is a thinly disguised eulogy. Without Tacitus's work, however, precious little would be known about Agricola. A fragmentary inscription from Verulamium records the building of the Forum in the town. Part of a name survives, the main element being IULIO ...GRIC, which is easily restored as Julius Agricola. His name is accompanied by the title PR.PR, indicating that he was pro-praetorian governor. Dating evidence derives from the fact that the Emperor Titus is described as the son of the divine Vespasian, so the inscription was set up after the death of Vespasian, which occurred in 79. This may be the actual year of the inscription, since the other vital piece of evidence concerns the number of years that Titus had held tribunician power, restored by archaeologists as VIIII (this number was not always written as IX), which makes the year of the Forum dedication 79, though an alternative reading has been suggested which would date it to 81. On lead pipes from the fortress at Chester, where the water supply was being installed, Agricola is named in full. These too are dated to 79, but Vespasian is still named as Emperor, so the pipes were laid down just before his death, which occurred on 24 June 79. Dating evidence doesn't get much closer than that.

If the inscription and the lead pipes were the only evidence for a governor named Gnaeus Julius Agricola, it would never be supposed that this man had already served in Britain twice, as tribune of a legion under Suetonius Paullinus, and as legate of XX legion under Cerialis. It would never be suggested that he held office for nearly seven years, since most governors served for about three years and then went on to other posts. It would be discerned from archaeological excavations that the Romans had reached Scotland and built some forts under the Flavian Emperors, but it would probably be assumed that there was more than one governor spanning this period. Agricola broke all the rules. It was not usual to carry out successive military appointments in the same province, and it was not usual to remain in post for such a long period. The most unusual factor is that a biography should have been compiled, and that it should have survived.

There is a wealth of information in Tacitus's work, but it does not contain all that historians and archaeologists need to know. There are no firm dates, so that there has been a perennial debate about when Agricola arrived and when he left. Tacitus writes of summer and winter seasons, alternating his accounts of military activity in the campaigning seasons with descriptions of civilian affairs in the winters. He gives few place names, only some of which are firmly identified, so that the task of marrying the archaeological discoveries to the text is fraught with difficulty. If the relevant sections of his *Histories* had survived, it may have been possible to corroborate and augment what is stated in the *Agricola*, but the books are lost. Nevertheless, the *Agricola* is invaluable. It is all we have, apart from Dio's few statements that are derived from Tacitus, and it must be remembered that Tacitus was not writing for an audience of archaeologists two thousand years in the future.

The dating controversy arises from the lack of knowledge as to when Agricola held the consulship. It would be a suffect consulship, taken up after the eponymous consuls stepped down, so the consular records do not record Agricola. Tacitus says Agricola entered his post as governor of Britain immediately after holding the consulship, so if he held it in 76, he would probably arrive in 77, and if he was consul in 77 then he would arrive in 78. This in turn affects the date when he left. In the end, it is probably an insoluble problem unless some startling piece of evidence turns up to settle the matter once and for all.

As soon as he arrived Agricola gathered the troops and set off for Wales, where the Ordovices had almost annihilated a cavalry unit. Tacitus says that it was late in the summer and the army was beginning to think about winter quarters, but this only emphasises Agricola's zeal and energy. After dealing with the Ordovices, he went on to Anglesey, where Suetonius had put in a garrison but was forced to leave when the rebellion of Boudicca broke out. The island had become a refuge for fugitives according to Tacitus, and in any case the conquest of Wales was not completed without a firm hold on Anglesey. It seems to have been a sudden decision to attack. The Britons were expecting ships to appear to ferry the soldiers across, but:

As usual with decisions taken at short notice, there were no ships available. The determination and energy of the general got the troops across [the straits]. He selected special auxiliaries who knew the fords, and whose native practice was to swim while carrying weapons and leading their horses. He told them to leave their equipment, and then threw them into the attack so suddenly that the enemy were astonished. They had been expecting an attack by sea, but now they saw that nothing was insuperable for men who waged war in this way. (Tacitus *Agricola* 18)

This passage sets the heroic tone for the rest of the governor's achievements. During the winter after the Welsh campaign, Agricola set about weeding out the various abuses that were inflicted on the Britons. Having served twice before in the province he presumably knew exactly what went on.

The second campaigning season was the first full one. Agricola gathered his army, as Tacitus says, which raises the question of where the troops came from. The legions were dispersed in the fortresses at Caerleon, Chester and York, which remained as legionary bases almost until the end of Roman Britain, and there may still have been a legion at Wroxeter. Several suggestions have been made as to which legions occupied these bases, but there is no absolute proof for any of the permutations. It is almost certain that II Augusta was at Caerleon, and IX Hispana was at York, but it is assumed that XX Valeria Victrix was at Wroxeter and II Adiutrix at Chester.

It is much more difficult to detect the location of the various auxiliary units, and to provide secure dates for the few forts that are known in the south. In order to assemble sufficient manpower for Cerialis's and Agricola's northern campaigns, it is suggested that some of the military posts in the south were given up, if not under Cerialis and Frontinus, then possibly now, as Agricola moved further north and established new forts. It is reasonable to suppose that some units were brought out of the garrisons of the south, and the process began of turning the evacuated forts into civilian developments. Likely candidates are Exeter, Cirencester, and Dorchester-on-Thames, but archaeological investigations suggest that civilian development in these places generally did not begin until about 80. The lack of buildings does not preclude a brief period of settlement inside the evacuated forts, but this is to go further than the evidence will allow. All that can be said is that Agricola founded a lot of forts in new areas, and he presumably drew the necessary soldiers from the south, which in turn implies that military government ceased in those areas and civilian government was established, but the details are lacking.

It is not clear where exactly Agricola aimed for in his second season. Tacitus says that Agricola was everywhere on the march and personally chose all the sites for pitching camp, dismissed as *topoi* by some modern authors, the usual sort of praise for an active general who harassed the enemy continually, raiding and attacking without let up. There is no hint as to where Agricola did all this. A more useful passage describes how the Romans entered new areas:

> As a result [of the campaigns] several states [*civitates*] which until then were used to acting independently gave up violence and sent hostages. They were surrounded by forts with such skill and thoroughness that no new part of Britain was won with so little damage. (Tacitus *Agricola* 20)

The reference to new areas suggests that Agricola was in southern Scotland, beyond the Brigantian territory that Cerialis had overrun. If Cerialis was the founder of the fort at Carlisle, then the forts that were so skilfully sited by Agricola ought to have been founded to the north of the Tyne–Solway line. Alternatively, it is possible that there was a need for consolidation in the hill country of the western Pennine area, which may not have been thoroughly pacified by Cerialis or Frontinus. This suggestion derives from the reference to forests and estuaries in Tacitus's description of the campaigns, but mention of forests and estuaries could easily apply to the west coast of southern Scotland, too, so it has to be said that no one knows the location of the 'new places' of Tacitus's description.

For the following year, the third campaigning season, which belongs to 79 if the early dating for Agricola's campaigns applies, there is an identifiable place name, or rather a river name, the Tay. Agricola marched '*usque ad Taum (aestuaria nomen est)*' says Tacitus, 'up to the Tay, which is the name of the estuary'. The Romans encountered new peoples (*novas gentes*), and Agricola built forts, which were occupied during the winter, distressing the natives who were used to fighting in summer and recouping their strengths in winter, but the new governor gave them no rest. Agricola needed to find a way to control groups of tribesmen who had no vested interest in risking a set battle, but could disperse and use their terrain for guerrilla warfare. He probably did it in the time-honoured brutal but effective way of preventing movement, attacking and burning crops and food stores in winter, and generally harassing the people:

> No fort established by Agricola was ever taken by storm or given up in surrender or retreat. The soldiers could make frequent raids and

were secure even if besieged because they had supplies to last for a whole year. The winter held no fears for them because they were self-sufficient, whereas the enemies were in despair because they were accustomed to recoup the losses of the summer by successes in the winter, but now they were given no rest in summer or winter. (Tacitus *Agricola* 22)

It was probably after these campaigns to conquer new peoples that the Emperor Titus was hailed as Imperator for the fifteenth time, in 79. Dio records this event after giving a short synopsis of Agricola's activities in Britain, not in chronological order but amalgamating different events without regard to their sequence. Dio specifically states that it was in connection with Agricola's achievements in Britain that Titus received the acclamation, but unfortunately he does not unequivocally relate the advance to the River Tay to the honours for the Emperor, which leaves considerable leeway for archaeologists to interpret the passage according to whichever dating is adopted for Agricola's arrival and departure. According to the later dating hypothesis, Titus's Imperial acclamation would belong to the fourth season, which was not one of campaigning and expanding the Empire, but one of consolidation, which seems a less likely achievement for Titus to celebrate, as opposed to the forward thrust of the previous year. The problem remains open to debate.

Consolidation: The Fourth Season AD 80

By his fourth season Agricola had overrun a large amount of new territory, and as Tacitus says, it was important to secure the recent conquests. Agricola spent the whole year on this task, before setting off on further expeditions. The consolidation probably extended from northern England to the 'new peoples' of Scotland that Agricola encountered in his third season. Tacitus says that in the fourth season, if only the glory of the army and the Roman name had allowed it, Agricola could have found an ideal place to call a halt (Tacitus calls it a *terminus*), between the estuaries of the Clyde and Forth, which he secured by planting garrisons (*praesidia*).

It is reasonable to assume that in consolidating his hold on the territory he had won, Agricola built forts up to this line, if not beyond it as far as the Tay. The problem is to identify where they were. In the past it was customary to assign to Agricola all the forts from Lancashire and Yorkshire up into Scotland, but as one scholar expressed it, this cannot be true, otherwise Agricola would have arrived at his final battle accompanied only by his batman. It is possible that Cerialis, Frontinus, and Agricola himself bypassed the Lake District, which seems to have been occupied at a later time, but the routes through and across the Pennines would require protection, so some forts were built to secure communications and supplies, as well as to keep control of the tribesmen. Forts which are definitely Agricolan in date are Lancaster, Ribchester and Brough–under-Stainmore. A map of Roman Britain with all known fort sites marked on it gives the impression that northern England was very closely guarded, but the forts were not all occupied at the same time, and without precise dating evidence, it cannot be said that Agricola built the entire network of forts in these areas.

One of the prime considerations in establishing Roman forts was the protection of routes. The forts at Carlisle in the west and Corbridge in the east almost certainly belong to Agricola's advance into Scotland though it is thought that Carlisle may already have been occupied under Cerialis a few years before. These forts would protect communication routes and provide supply bases for the northern advance. At Corbridge the Agricolan fort was not built on the site of the remains exhibited today on the edge of the modern town, but at the Red House site some short distance away. This fort was discovered when the modern A69 was being constructed, to take traffic away from the town. It has been interpreted as a supply base on account of the open-ended shed-like structures found there. Nothing similar has been found at Carlisle, where the fort identified as Agricolan is too small to suggest that it functioned in the same way.

From Northumberland and Cumbria into Scotland there were two main routes, Dere Street in the east leading up to the Forth, and in the west the road ran through Annandale to the Clyde. Forts were built to protect these routes, though on the principle that Roman forts were usually situated at intervals of about one day's march, it seems that not all of them have been discovered. On the west side the fort at Dalswinton was the largest and most important. There are two successive forts on this site, each with two phases of occupation. One of the two-phase forts is definitely dated to the Flavian period, while the other is not dated but it is situated in a less well chosen position, which probably indicates that this fort was built first, and then a better site close by was chosen for a second fort. Since it seems unlikely that Agricola was responsible for all four phases of occupation, either his predecessors Cerialis or Frontinus were there before him, or his unknown successor occupied the area after him. The fort at Loudoun Hill also has four phases of occupation, which could perhaps be explained in the same way. It is tempting to link the supposedly earlier phases with Cerialis's drive to the north during his campaign in Brigantia, but up to now there is no firm evidence to support the theory.

On the eastern side of the country, the fort at Newstead was built in close proximity to the three Eildon Hills, from which it takes its Roman name of Trimontium. The three hills have to be viewed from a particular angle to see that there are indeed three peaks, one of which looks as though it is struggling to get away from the other two. On Eildon Hill North, a Roman watchtower was built, in the middle of what is considered to be the tribal capital of the Selgovae. This implies that the tribe was hostile and required close supervision. It is usually considered that the neighbouring tribe of the Novantae were also hostile. By contrast, the Votadini of the eastern coastal strip seem to have been friendly to the Romans. This tribe occupied their stronghold of Traprain Law through the Roman occupation, and few forts have come to light in the territory of the Votadini, implying that there was no need to guard it closely.

Tacitus's statement that in the fourth season Agricola had found an ideal *terminus* for his conquests is exact enough to locate it on a small-scale map, running across the country between the Forth and Clyde, but on the larger scale it proves to be very irritating, because up to now there is very little indication of where the *praesidia* were established between the Forth and Clyde. Like all the forts in Britain at this time, these *praesidia* would be built of turf and timber, and so traces of them may have been superseded or obliterated by later buildings, or perhaps were not recognised during nineteenth-century excavations, but even so it seems that Agricola's forts were not all built on exactly the same sites as the those of the Antonine Wall, which also connected the two estuaries in the second century. The only indication that Agricola may have chosen some of the sites that were occupied in the Antonine period derives not from archaeological traces of fort walls or buildings, but from the artefacts of Flavian date found at Cadder, Castlecary and Mumrills.

The forts of Flavian date at Mollins and Camelon, and more recent discovery of a Flavian fort at Doune, suggest that Agricola's potential *terminus* was never intended to run along the same line as the Antonine Wall. His criteria would be slightly different. Although one of the prime considerations would be the control of movement, he was not looking for suitable geographical terrain on which to build a running barrier, like the Antonine turf wall with forts strung out along it. Frontiers of this solid kind were not the fashion in Agricola's day, but the Flavian system for guarding the borders of Germany consisted of a road with watch towers, and though there is no absolutely precise dating evidence for this system, it was perhaps contemporary with Agricola. He would site his forts in places where the garrisons could keep watch over the surrounding area, send out patrols, guard communications and supplies, and control movement up and down the north–south routes to his rear, as well as east to west.

In the west, the fort at Barochan Hill was probably part of the Agricolan *terminus*, watching over the estuary of the Clyde, while Elginhaugh fulfilled the same purpose on the eastern side. The fort at Elginhaugh yielded high-quality Flavian finds, suggesting that it may have been Agricola's headquarters. It may not be wholly by accident that in the seventeenth century, when General Monck administered Scotland under Cromwell, he set up his headquarters at Dalkeith, not far from Elginhaugh.

One of the major problems of matching the known military installations to Tacitus's narrative is the date of the forts at Ardoch and Strageath and the road and watchtowers running along the Gask Ridge around the western edge of Fife. Since dating evidence is not sufficiently precise to pinpoint the foundation dates with any certainty, these forts and towers could belong to any of Agricola's campaigning seasons from the fourth to the seventh, or indeed to the period after he had been recalled. However, Tacitus is unequivocal in his description of the third season, when he says that Agricola reached

the Tay. The towers of the Gask Ridge ran from Ardoch to the fort at
Bertha on the Tay. It is permissible to speculate that there may have
been more towers, not yet discovered, on the road south of Ardoch
as far as Camelon, which would join the towers and forts of the
Gask Ridge to the *praesidia* of the *terminus*. In that case it is possible
that the forts at Ardoch, Strageath and Bertha and the postulated
intervening towers were built to guard the route to the north as part
of the consolidation process of the fourth season, when Agricola
would have time and manpower because he and his army were not
engaged in major campaigns. This suggestion is unorthodox, since a
later date is usually favoured for these forts and towers.

The Fifth to the Seventh Seasons AD 81 to 83

If the fifth season occupied the summer of 81, as it does according to
the earlier dating for Agricola's tenure of Britain, then the order, or the
permission, to resume the advance after the fourth season's halt came
from the Emperor Titus. In September 81 Titus died, so according to
the scenario of the later dating, the halt on the Forth–Clyde line and
the building of forts was carried out in the final months of Titus's
reign. In this case the fifth season and the advance beyond the Forth–
Clyde line began in 82, so the order to resume the conquest would
emanate from the Emperor Domitian, Titus's brother.

At the opening of the fifth season's campaigns, Agricola may have
concentrated on western Scotland. Tacitus describes how the general
'crossed in the first ship', in other words leading from the front in a
combined ops manoeuvre with the fleet and the army. The problem is
that there is no mention of what he crossed. The only clue is that the
army arrived at the point where Scotland faces Ireland, which places
him firmly in the west, and it has been argued that since Tacitus
mentions the Forth and the Clyde in the previous season, it ought to
be the River Clyde that Agricola crossed. The part of Scotland which
faces Ireland is taken to mean the Mull of Kintyre, but it has also
been argued that in his fifth season Agricola was indeed operating in
the west, but much further south in Galloway. On the grounds that
the Romans marched past the Lake District and garrisoned it later,
it is suggested that this area had been ignored in the initial advance

into Scotland, and Agricola needed to consolidate before he marched further north.

There is hardly any detail in Tacitus's work about the events of the fifth season. Great attention is paid to Ireland instead of Scotland, starting with the Irish king who arrived at Agricola's headquarters after being thrown out of his kingdom in a family squabble. Agricola gave some thought to the conquest of Ireland, which he thought would require one legion and some auxiliaries. Anyone from the time of Henry II in the twelfth century to the Earl of Essex in the sixteenth would be able to point out that the Irish tribes might be primitive, but it would prove very difficult to pin then down and defeat them. For the Romans, of course, it remained a passing fancy, and Agricola turned back to Scotland.

For the final two seasons, leading up to the great Battle of Mons Graupius, Tacitus devotes many more words and provides more detail than he does for the previous seasons. It makes no difference now whether the early or late dating for Agricola's governorship is used, since in either case the final two-year run-up to the Battle of Mons Graupius took place under Domitian. After so many seasons in Britain, Agricola may have anticipated that he would be recalled, but it seems that Domitian was satisfied with what had been achieved so far and authorised Agricola to continue along the same lines. So the sixth season was spent north of the Forth, concentrating on the eastern side of the country, and working in co-operation with the fleet, reconnoitring the harbours. The fleet was also used to make sudden raids from the coast, to spread terror and perhaps inspire the Britons to fight. In northern Scotland, the natives did not need to risk a battle, but could retreat into the mountains and wait until invaders went away, so in the sixth season Agricola failed to bring about the final conflict. Tacitus describes how the tribesmen retaliated:

The people of Caledonia started to arm themselves. They made great preparations, which were exaggerated by rumour. They caused alarm by attacking some forts, as though they were provoking [the Romans]. There were some cowardly men [in Agricola's army] who advised that it would be safer to retreat behind the Forth rather than be driven back. In the interim, Agricola found out that the enemy was about to attack in large numbers, so to avoid being surrounded

by forces who outnumbered his own and knew the terrain, he split
his army into three groups and advanced. (Tacitus *Agricola* 25)

One of these three army groups was attacked and nearly defeated. The
tribesmen (Caledonians, but Tacitus does not call them by this name,
preferring to use the phrase 'the people of Caledonia') knew that the
IX legion was understrength and was therefore the weakest of the three
groups. The lack of manpower may have arisen because a vexillation
had been sent to Germany, where Domitian was preparing for a war
against the fierce Chatti. Alternatively, there may have been a need for a
number of legionaries from IX to remain at their base at York to keep a
watch on northern England. Whatever the reason, the knowledge that
IX legion was weak implies good intelligence on the part of the Britons,
who launched a night attack, creeping up to the Roman camp, where
they quickly despatched the sentries and burst in, slaughtering as they
went. Agricola had posted scouts who informed him that the Britons
were on the move, heading for the camp of the IX legion. Agricola
seems to have been on the march even before the Britons reached their
destination and began their assault, but by the time he and the Roman
troops arrived, the IX legion was in tremendous difficulties. But now
the Britons were caught between two armies, one in the camp and one
coming to its relief. The tribesmen were thrown out, but there was
no pursuit, and the Britons disappeared into the forests and marshes.
Tacitus says that if the tribesmen had not been aided by their terrain
which covered their escape, the war could have been concluded.

This Roman victory spurred on the soldiers, who were impressed
with their own achievements and now clamoured to be led to the
furthest parts of the country. Even the ones who had advised retreat
were all fired up and eager to march. One wonders who these sudden
fire-eating converts were, and if Agricola reminisced to his son-in-law
about them through clenched teeth. Somehow, the enthusiasm of the
troops had to be maintained over the winter, since the advance to the
north did not begin immediately.

There was an interesting event at the end of the sixth season, when
the recently recruited tribesmen of the Germanic Usipi, who had
been forcibly enlisted and sent to join the Roman army in Britain,
decided that they no longer wanted to be Roman soldiers, and they
resolved to set off for home. They killed their officers, stole some

ships and set sail, but the winds and the tides took them all the way
around the island, and they ended up on the same side of Britain
where they had started. Their fate was worse than serving as soldiers,
since many of them starved to death and the ones who survived were
sold as slaves when they fetched up on the coast near the territory of
the Frisii. Their exploits had important consequences for the Romans.
For the first time, there was proof that Britain was an island, officially
confirmed later on when Agricola's fleet circumnavigated the whole
country and the participants were able to report what the northern
seas were like. The sailors observed that in the late summer the sun
did not set in the most northerly parts, but simply skirted the horizon
for a short time and then started to rise again.

The final push to conquer Scotland began in Agricola's seventh and
last season. His family was with him in Britain, and at the beginning
of the summer, his infant son died, but Tacitus says that he bore the
loss well, and the coming campaign provided a distraction for him.
The tribes had been making preparations to meet the threat that they
knew was coming, and had at last formed alliances and chosen a leader,
just as the Britons of the south chose Cassivellanus to co-ordinate the
campaigns against Julius Caesar. The leader of the Caledonian tribes
was Calgacus, renowned for his bravery and nobility, as his name, or
rather his title attests: he was 'the Swordsman'. He assembled 30,000
warriors, which seems a high figure for a sparsely populated area, but
it is not known where the limits of his recruiting grounds lay.

Apart from the report that the fleet was used for plundering raids and
attacks from the coast, Tacitus does not provide much detail about how
the Romans arrived at Mons Graupius, where the final battle occurred.
The description of the battle itself, and the speeches of the Roman
general and the Caledonian leader before it took place, occupy a large
proportion of the whole work. Hints as to what the Roman army did
on the way to the battle and where they were when it was fought have
to be gleaned from the words that Tacitus invents for these speeches.

The Search for Mons Graupius

The puzzle of Mons Graupius will probably never be solved. It has
to be located near a mountain, which for Scotland does not narrow

the choice very much. There is a consistent mindset among some scholars that casts doubt on the ability of Agricola and his army to get very far into Scotland, so it is suggested that this final battle must have been fought on the flank of the Highlands, certainly not in the interior of the mountain zone, and probably not much further north than Aberdeen. One of the more recent suggestions for the battle site is at Bennachie, where there is a very large Roman marching camp at Durno that could have held Agricola's forces as he assembled them for battle. But until more evidence comes to light, it is not certain that this suggestion is any more valid than any other mountain location.

Any suggestion that the battle may have been fought in the Highlands is dismissed with a snort of derision. The main problem is that no traces of Roman camps and forts have been found further north than the Great Glen, and those that have been found are all located on the edge of the Highlands, guarding the routes through the glens into and out of the mountains, so it is considered inconceivable that the Romans ever set foot in the Highlands, at least before the main battle was fought, and probably not even after the Romans had won it. The forts at the mouths of the glens are considered to be springboards for further attacks into the mountains to round up the tribesmen after the great Battle of Mons Graupius.

It is worth pointing out that other armies which conquered Scotland found it necessary to go into the Highlands to persuade the natives to fight, and to remain there to stop them from gathering. It has been said that in Scotland it is the invaders who starve while the natives take to the mountains and wait. In the seventeenth century, General Monck led his troops all over the mountain passes, on routes which even the natives said their forefathers never used. Nearly a century later the Hanoverians placed garrisons in the mountains. Scotland is not conquered unless the Highlands are controlled, and while it could be argued that Agricola or his successor had achieved this by establishing forts at the glen mouths, the important point is that it is a considerable achievement to persuade the Britons to fight a pitched battle, risking everything on a single chance to win. It suggests that Agricola had gone into the Highlands to flush the tribesmen out, making it impossible for them to find refuge there, burning and destroying settlements and food supplies, and so ensuring that the Britons had nothing left to lose by fighting him.

When compared and contrasted with the campaigns of the Emperors Septimius Severus and Caracalla at the beginning of the third century, Agricola's achievement in bringing about a major battle is of supreme importance. Although Severus planned very thoroughly for his campaigns, ensuring supplies for the troops and combining land operations with the fleet, he did not bring about a decisive battle. Dio says that Severus never fought a battle and never saw the enemy drawn up in battle lines, and Herodian emphasises how easy it was for the tribesmen to run off and hide. After the campaigns of Severus and Caracalla, there was peace for some years, but the country was not occupied and held down as it was under Agricola and the succeeding Flavian governors.

Apart from scepticism that Agricola conducted any military operations in the Highlands, similarly the idea that Agricola, or indeed Severus, could have reached the ultimate northern coast is also dismissed. But if Agricola stopped short of the extreme end of the island he had not conquered the whole of it, and the fact that he had not reached the ultimate shore would be clear to all the soldiers who took part, not to mention any observers who were with the army, like the Greek scholar Demetrius of Tarsus, who sailed with the fleet to some of the islands that surround Britain. Demetrius may be the same man as Scribonius Demetrius, who made two dedications at York, one to the gods of the governor's headquarters, and one to Ocean and Tethys, both of them quite appropriate if he was attached to Agricola's entourage and went on sea voyages with the fleet.

Despite the belief that Agricola never reached the ultimate northern coast, a case has been made by one or two scholars for locating the final Battle of Mons Graupius in the northernmost part of Scotland. It was late in the season when it was fought, which suggests that there had been a long march to arrive there, corroborated by Tacitus's version of Agricola's speech to the troops, which in turn indicates that the long march had not taken the Romans around in circles but had brought the troops directly to the far north. More important, the speech that Tacitus invents for the leader Calgacus implies that there was nowhere else to go:

> There is no land beyond us, and even the sea provides no refuge
> because we are threatened by the fleet … we are the last people on

earth, the last free men, we live in a remote land known only by rumour, and this has protected us until today. The farthest point of Britain is open … there are no people beyond us, only sea and rock. (Tacitus *Agricola* 30)

The debate about the location of Mons Graupius will be a perennial one, but at least it can generate enthusiasm and scholarship, possibly more so than if Tacitus had been able to give a complete modern grid reference to the site. Archaeological finds may one day reveal the place, just as the site of the *Varusschlacht* has been found in Germany, where the Roman legions of Quinctilius Varus were wiped out by Arminius in AD 9.

The description of the preliminaries to the battle and the combat itself occupy several pages in Tacitus's account. The fighting took place on the slope of a hill, where Calgacus's warriors formed up. Agricola put his legions in reserve and fought the entire battle employing only his auxiliaries. The cavalry attended to the British chariots while the Batavians and Tungrians attacked the main force, but the Britons began to move down the hill in an attempt to get round the Roman rear. Agricola had kept some cavalry in reserve, so he threw them into the fighting. They managed to break through the ranks of the tribesmen and then come round to attack them from behind. This trapped the warriors between the horsemen and the Roman infantry units, so there was great slaughter, amounting to 10,000 Britons according to Tacitus. Only 360 Romans were killed.

Next day there were no Britons to be found, which suggests that they had gone to ground in the mountains and valleys. Technically it was not such a complete victory as Tacitus claims on behalf of his father -in-law, since a large number of tribesmen were still alive and free, and the task of extracting them from the mountains would be labour-intensive. It was late in the season, and Agricola did not try to pursue and round up the warriors. It is not known if he made any treaty arrangements with the tribes, although he did take some hostages, suggesting that there may have been some sort of dialogue. He marched slowly back towards the south, to impress the Britons by his nonchalant progress. The fleet was ordered to sail round the island, allocating some troops to the prefect in command of the ships. Then he put the army into winter quarters.

After Agricola

Agricola was probably recalled in 84, perhaps using the winter following the battle to begin the process of consolidation of the Roman hold on the north. Tacitus says that Agricola handed over a peaceful province to his successor, who may have been Sallustius Lucullus. He is attested as governor at some unknown time, but it is not clear when he arrived in the province. Very little is known about events in Britain after Agricola's departure. The man who had completed the conquest of Britain could look forward to honours and further important appointments, but instead he was ignored, a point which Tacitus emphasises on behalf of his father-in-law. He suggests that the lack of promotion was due to Domitian's suspicion and jealousy. There may be some partial truth in the accusation, but no one knows why Agricola, the British specialist, was not called upon to carry out any further tasks. He had hoped to be made governor of Syria, but the offer never came, and he died, probably in 93, a disappointed man. Three years later, Domitian was assassinated, and a short time after that, when everyone could breathe freely again, Tacitus started work on his biographical tribute to his father-in-law. If he had not done so, the mystery of Flavian Scotland would hinge on a jumble of forts and camps around the Highland fringe, and on the routes to and from northern England.

The Camps and Forts of Agricola's Campaigns

Attempts have been made to trace the movements of Agricola's army on campaign by assigning the known temporary camps to individual seasons. On the march, the Roman troops traditionally built a camp every time they halted for the night, by digging a ditch and throwing the earth inside the perimeter to create a rampart. On top of this they often placed wooden stakes to form a palisade. Such temporary camps are notoriously difficult to date, though a line of camps, evenly spaced and more or less the same size can indicate the route that an army followed, but that is about all. Questions as to the direction of the march, whose army they belonged to and when they were built, can very rarely be answered. There were at least four major campaigns in Scotland under different governors or Emperors. Agricola campaigned in the first century, and in the mid-second century the governor Lollius Urbicus fought battles in the north in the reign of Antoninus Pius. At the beginning of the third century Roman armies campaigned probably up to the far north under the personal direction of the Emperor Severus. Another foray into Scotland took place under Constantius at the beginning of the fourth century, but even less is known about his achievements than about the other campaigns. Without secure dating evidence, the various series of camps that have been found could belong to any of these campaign armies.

There are only a few camps that can definitely be assigned to Agricola. There are two very large square camps at Dunning and Abernethy that could have held a campaign force on the march, and these are usually assigned to Agricola's army. The so-called Stracathro camps, named after the place where the first example was discovered, can be attributed to Agricola with more certainty. These camps have very distinctive gateways, with a curving bank and ditch projecting outwards around one half of the gate. This is called a *clavicula*, and examples are known from other provinces. The aim was to force anyone entering the camp to turn his unshielded side towards the defenders. The Stracathro camps are quite distinct because in addition to the curving bank and ditch they also display a second projecting arm, emerging from the opposite side of the gate, running straight towards the end of the curve, leaving a narrow gap between the two. No such camps have been found in Britain except in the Flavian period, and they are not found at all in other provinces. It suggests that Agricola himself had a hand in designing them.

There are six known Stracathro type camps, all near forts that were presumably built a short time later. They vary in size. Only the two on the east of the Highlands at Auchinhove and Ythan Wells are large enough to hold a substantial force. The others are at the mouths of some of the glens leading out of the Highlands to the southern lowlands. As such, they probably do not mark a line of march round the southern edge of the Highlands, but they most likely represent a temporary arrangement to watch the glens and the traffic into and out of them, while Agricola finally rounded up the Britons and brought them to battle. The main objection is that such an arrangement would reduce his available manpower when it came to the final battle, but on the other hand if he penetrated to the far north, he may have thought it more important to ensure that the tribes did not take to the mountains, march through the glens, and come down behind him.

As for the permanent forts in Scotland beyond the Forth–Clyde line, these may have been planned, or even founded by Agricola himself, but it is possible that he did not have enough time to complete them all, and that it was his unknown successor as governor who finished what Agricola had begun. Like the forts further south, most of these installations would be built of turf and timber. A fort was planted at the mouth of each of the Highland glens, with the legionary fortress of Inchtuthil guarding the most important route through the valley of the River Tay. From west to east, the other forts are Barochan on the Clyde, Drumquhassle, Menteith, Bochastle, Dalginross, Fendoch, Cargill (which lies south-east of the legionary fortress), the two larger forts at Cardean and Stracathro, with a small fortlet at Inverquharity guarding a minor route between these two. There may be more forts awaiting discovery, but despite efforts to identify Agricolan installations continuing around the eastern edge of the Highlands and up to the Moray Firth, nothing has yet been confirmed. One of the difficulties is the short time that any such forts would have been in occupation, and another is that some of the rivers in Scotland can change course in severe floods, so it is possible that vital evidence has been washed away.

The occupants of the legionary fortress at Inchtuthil are not attested. It is suggested that it was XX Valeria Victrix, while II Adiutrix was at Chester. The other forts would be most likely manned by auxiliary units, but possibly not in a neat arrangement with one discrete unit allocated to each fort. Mixed garrisons may have been stationed in the forts, combining cavalry and infantry, as was the case later on at Newstead and possibly Dalswinton. It is not known for certain how the glen-blocking forts worked, but it is reasonable to suppose that the troops patrolled the glens to the north and the lowland areas to the south, more along the lines of police work than military operations. It is usually considered that the forts were springboards for the penetration and pacification of the Highlands, but there is no evidence that the Romans adopted these measures. However they functioned, the units of the Highland line, and the garrisons of the forts on the roads to the south, were not given more than a few years to practise their technique before they were withdrawn.

Scotland Immediately Let Go

Tacitus's famous phrase, *perdomita Britannia, statim missa* (Britain was conquered and immediately let go) is a bitter indictment of the Emperor Domitian, on behalf of Agricola. It could be questioned whether Britannia was really *perdomita*, but it seems that *statim missa* is not quite the exaggeration that it was once thought. Tacitus was accused of exaggerating, because the older theories regarding the abandonment of Scotland were based on the probability of a gradual phased withdrawal, but it now seems that the first-century occupation of Scotland was indeed very short. It appears that around 87, the glen-blocking forts and the legionary fortress at Inchtuthil were abandoned. The evidence for the date derives from coins. Excavations at Stracathro and Inchtuthil produced bronze *asses* of 86, but nothing later than this date. These bronze coins were the small change used to pay the soldiers, whose cash wages were reduced to a small sum after the deductions had been made for food and clothing, any lost or damaged equipment, compulsory savings, the burial club, and other items. The fact that the bronze *asses* of 86 were all in mint condition means that they had not been in circulation for very long. No coins of a later date have turned up at any of glen forts, even though bronze coins of 87 and later dates reached forts further south in quantity.

The coin evidence, taken together with the fact that the forts at Fendoch and Mollins – and the legionary fortress of Inchtuthil – were deliberately and tidily demolished, suggests that the Romans left the whole area precipitately, and that all units were withdrawn at the same time. The legionary fortress had not even been completed, and the Romans buried over a million nails there, in preference to packing them up and transporting them, and definitely in preference to allowing the natives access to so much iron.

The reason for the withdrawal was the war on the Danube. The Dacians had erupted into the Roman province of Moesia, defeated the Roman troops and killed the governor. The Emperor Domitian assembled another army under the Praetorian Prefect Fuscus. The Dacians defeated this army as well. The Danube provinces were much closer to Rome than Britain was, and therefore much more of a threat, so when Domitian prepared for a third war, the soldiers from Britain would provide some of the necessary manpower. The Emperor spent much of the year 87 in preparation for the new campaign, so this ties in well with the postulated date of 87 for the withdrawal of troops from Scotland. II Adiutrix may have been removed at the same time, though it is not attested in Moesia until 92. If the legion left Chester as XX Valeria Victrix was marching from Inchtuthil, there would have been a smooth evacuation and reoccupation of the Chester fortress. If there was any delay, the Wroxeter fortress may have been used to house the extra troops. But it is more plausible that Domitian ordered II Adiutrix to leave Britain in 87, rather than shuffling them about unnecessarily.

Probably at the same time that Inchtuthil and the glen forts were abandoned, the forts at Newstead and Dalswinton were enlarged to take more troops. A mint coin of 86 was found at Newstead in the ditch of the first fort, which had been filled in as the new fort was built. The new garrison was probably mixed, consisting of legionaries and auxiliary cavalry, and at Dalswinton there may have been two cavalry units. It has been suggested that the forts at Ardoch and Strageath, and the Gask towers belong to the withdrawal phase rather than the period when the Romans were advancing, but it seems needlessly laborious and time-consuming to build forts simply to organise protection of the area during a phased withdrawal, which is in any case discredited by the coin evidence of a rapid and complete evacuation, leaving nothing beyond the Forth–Clyde line. It is certain that nothing north of this line was occupied after 90, but the finer details of which forts were still in use between the Forth–Clyde line and Newstead and Dalswinton are more difficult to discern.

The years between 90 and the assassination of the Emperor Domitian in 96 are very dark in more ways than one. In Britain, these are dark years because there is hardly a glimmer of information to illuminate what happened in the final decade of the first century. Only one governor is known for certain, Sallustius Lucullus, who may have been Agricola's successor. He did not survive for long. The official story was that he had had the temerity to invent a new spear and name it the Lucullan, after himself, so he was executed on Domitian's orders. There may be more to the story. He may have been involved somehow in the revolt of the Rhine legions under the governor Saturninus in 89, or perhaps Domitian merely thought he was, and that was enough to warrant his execution.

During the dark years at the end of Domitian's reign everyone in Rome lived in fear of the increasingly paranoid Emperor. After the revolt of Saturninus, Domitian became ever more suspicious of the senators. He feared assassination so much that he had the palace corridors lined with polished slabs of stone so that he could see in their mirror-like surfaces if anyone was coming up behind him. He started to execute people on the merest hint of conspiracy or treason. He may have been suspicious of Agricola, whose achievements in Britain had after all earned his brother the Emperor Titus an Imperial acclamation. Agricola was spared from any accusations of disloyalty by dying before the Emperor. Three years afterwards, Domitian was stabbed to death by his secretary. The senators claimed that they had no complicity in the plot, and appointed one of their own respected members, Cocceius Nerva, as Emperor. He was already of advanced age, and died after only two years, but he had adopted as his successor the successful general Trajan, who became Emperor in 98.

Civilian Development under the Flavian Governors

During the Flavian era in southern Britain, a great surge of building works and town development has been detected wherever archaeological excavations have taken place. No town has yet been shown to possess a Forum and basilica before Flavian times, with the possible exception of Silchester, part of Togidubnus's kingdom, where a timber building dated *c.*50 was found underneath the late first-century Forum, but it is not certain whether this first building should be identified as a predecessor to the Forum. At other towns development of civic buildings is persistently Flavian in date. It might be expected that at Canterbury, where Claudian buildings have been found, there would be an early establishment of a Forum and basilica, but even here, among the most Romanised tribe, the

Cantiaci, development is still Flavian. Similarly, in London, where the administrative headquarters of the procurator and most probably the governor were located, public buildings also seem to be lacking until the Flavian period.

It is all too easy to attribute all this building work to the influence of Agricola, because Tacitus says that this is what he did:

> His [Agricola's] plan was to urge the primitive people who lived in scattered settlements, and were inclined to make war, to become accustomed to peace and quiet and the pleasurable life. For this reason he encouraged individuals and advised communities to build temples, Forums, and houses, by praising the people who were eager and castigating the laggards, and as a result people competed for honours instead of having to be coerced. (Tacitus *Agricola* 21)

Tacitus's statement that Agricola encouraged the Britons to move from their scattered settlements and build Forums and basilicas, temples and houses, is the most unequivocal evidence for persuading, but not actively coercing, the Britons to embrace the Roman way of life, though the passage carefully ignores the achievements of Agricola's predecessors. The theory that Romanisation was deliberately fostered by the government and spread by the army is now discredited. In the southern half of Britain, military occupation was much reduced towards the end of the first century, and yet this was the area where Romanisation rapidly developed after the army withdrew, whereas the military forces occupied the more northerly parts of Britain in great strength and for a long period, but most of the natives continued to live in Iron Age-style roundhouses throughout the Roman era.

A more rational view of the Flavian advances in civic life would be to attribute at least some of the work to Cerialis and in particular Frontinus. The establishment of civil settlements at Exeter, Cirencester, and especially at Caerwent, might be his work. Chichester, Winchester and Silchester were probably Romanised initially by Togidubnus, but like other towns they received their public buildings in the late Flavian period, and may be associated with Agricola, or his successor. Only at Verulamium can the building of a Forum be definitely connected to Agricola. The inscription recording the dedication of the Forum complex bears his name, but the original impetus for the building could have started under Frontinus. The date of the inscription is interpreted as either 79 or 81, so if the first alternative is correct, it is questionable whether the building could have been planned and finished wholly in Agricola's tenure of office, since he arrived in the late summer of 77, which allows only two years for the initiation of the building to its completion. The later dating for his appointment as governor places his arrival in 78, which would make the timescale of only one year even more improbable.

The design of the Forum at Verulamium is reminiscent of the headquarters building of a Roman fort, with an open square in the centre, enclosed on three sides by a colonnade, and on the fourth side by the offices, or in the civilian version, the basilica, usually an aisled building with the centre section raised above the aisle or aisles, so that the windows of the higher walls provide light inside the building. The question is, who built the Forum at Verulamium, and at other towns? It is conceivable that military engineers could advise on the projects during the winters, and perhaps some legionaries could have helped with the work, but while the three Flavian governors were constantly engaged in warfare it is doubtful if there would be enough manpower to be able lend some men to supervise building work in the towns. For those towns which developed in the late Flavian period, the military may have assisted, since the far north was abandoned, and even though several auxiliary units and a legion had been removed for Domitian's wars, there may have been enough experienced soldiers with time on their hands.

Apart from administrative buildings, some towns acquired other public establishments in the Flavian period, for entertainment and religious practices. There was a theatre at Colchester before 60, and Canterbury acquired one *c*.80. At Verulamium, it appears that a site was prepared for a theatre in Flavian times but there was no building work until the mid-second century, unless flimsy temporary structures were erected for various performances and then demolished, as was customary in Rome itself, until Pompey the Great built the first permanent theatre in stone in the first century BC. Amphitheatres were built outside several towns, though these are mostly dated to post-Flavian times. Silchester possessed a timber amphitheatre probably as early as 55, and at Cirencester a disused quarry was converted into an amphitheatre. These structures may have been used in all towns for many more diverse events than combat between gladiators and the slaughter of animals. Festivals, processions and religious observances may have taken place in them.

One of the more important establishments in any Roman town was the bath house, and eventually the British towns acquired one or more bath complexes. At least two sets of public baths were built in London at the end of the first century, but Silchester already possessed a bathing establishment in the 50s.

It is unlikely that the Roman government helped to finance the establishment of civic buildings, temples, theatres, amphitheatres and baths, so the cash would have to be raised by the leading Britons. The desultory development of towns in the first decades of the Roman occupation may be explained in part by the impoverishment of many tribes after the suppression of the Boudiccan rebellion. Only a few tribes already used coinage when the Romans invaded, so for the rest the introduction by the Romans of a completely different economic system to their own may have set some British elite groups at a disadvantage.

The encouragement of the Britons to establish towns, enabling the Britons to enjoy the Roman way of life, was not entirely altruistic on the part of the Romans. One of the more pressing reasons was the need to devolve local government onto the British communities to relieve the pressure on the provincial administration. It is possible that the British tribes had already started to govern themselves without the appurtenances of elaborate buildings, but once the Forum and basilica appeared in a town it can be taken as a sure sign that there was also a town council and magistrates to carry out the functions of government, to administer the law and supervise the tax collection within their boundaries. The town officials may have used their native language for day-to-day business, but Latin was the language for dealing with the Romans, for administration, finance and law. Agricola encouraged the spread of Latin and literacy, and took a personal interest in the education of the sons of the British elite. He considered that the Britons possessed a greater natural ability than the Gauls, which suggests that he had talked to some of them and observed them at close quarters. On the whole, what Tacitus says about Agricola's contribution to the development of Britain should not be dismissed merely as eulogistic hyperbole.

Another aspect of civil development is the appointment of *legati iuridici* to Britain. These officials were appointed by the Emperor, and were first introduced by Vespasian. It is suggested that *iuridici* were appointed during periods when the governor was fully occupied on military campaigns. Two are known from the Flavian period: Gaius Salvius Liberalis, who was in Britain from 78 to 81 while Agricola was engaged on his northern campaigns, and Lucius Javolenus Priscus, attested in Britain from 84 to 86. Both these men were of praetorian rank and had commanded legions. Their functions would be primarily the administration of justice, and to handle all aspects of legal work which the governor on campaign could not attend to personally. They may also have been involved in the development of new towns, helping to set up their administrative systems, advising on rights and privileges, and the duties and obligations of the inhabitants and the town councils. For the first generation of town councillors, the proceedings would be something of a culture shock, no matter how much contact they may already have had with Roman goods and the Roman way of life. There would be a period of initiation into a different way of governing their people. Nowadays, when so many systems are changing as computerisation grows ever more important, and one person performs the tasks that three people used to carry out, there are counsellors who can advise workers who have to cope with changes to the way in which they operate. The *legati iuridici* may have been called upon to facilitate the transition from tribal rule to Roman administration.

Civitas Capitals

The *civitas* (plural *civitates*) is sometimes translated as state, but it does not imply anything as large or sophisticated as the modern version of a state. *Civitas* was the term used by the Romans in less well developed areas to describe the territory of a tribe, implying a unit of local government. The word is related to *civis*, citizen, but this does not automatically indicate Roman citizenship. The *civitates* of Britain were inhabited by non-Romans, and would be called *civitates peregrinae*. Archaeologists invented the term *civitas* capitals to describe the towns of Roman Britain where the headquarters of local administration were centred, though this simple generalisation is subject to much debate.

Evidence for the existence of *civitas* capitals in Britain derives from some inscriptions, which unfortunately do not provide any firm dating evidence, and there is more information in two Roman documents. One of these documents is the *Antonine Itinerary*, a list of roads, naming towns along each of its routes, dating from the end of the second or beginning of the third century AD. The second document is the *Ravenna Cosmography*, a work of the seventh century, but for its British sections, the compilers used information that was well out of date, derived from the second-century situation in Britain. The places listed in these two documents are not precisely the same, but to a large extent they corroborate each other, and the documents also corroborate some of the inscriptions, of which there are eleven that concern *civitas* capitals. Five of these came from Wroxeter, Cirencester, Kenchester, Brougham and Caerwent, and the remaining six were found on Hadrian's Wall, where the *civitates* contributed to rebuilding work, at some unknown date. This was possibly at the beginning of the third century, in the reign of Severus, when the Wall was extensively repaired.

The *civitas* capitals were usually distinguished by a place name attached to a tribal suffix, such as Corinium Dobunnorum, or Corinium of the Dobunni, now called Cirencester, or Venta Silurum, Venta of the Silures, modern Caerwent. In most cases the tribal names have not survived into modern times, in contrast to some places on the Continent. In Gaul, for instance, Lutetia Parisiorum became Paris, not Lutece, which is reserved by modern historians for the ancient Roman version of the city. Only the Cantiaci of Durovernum Cantiacorum are still traceable in Britain, in Canterbury. The other towns usually preserve only the first part of the Roman place name. Winchester, which started out as Venta Belgarum, combines a corrupted version of Venta without the tribal name, but with the addition of the suffix '-chester', derived from the Roman *castra*. The same contraction is represented by Caerwent in south Wales, where the first half of Venta Silurum is combined with the Welsh version of *castra*, Caer, or Gaer. Similarly if you say Coriniumcastra fast enough for long enough with an approximation of an Anglo-Saxon inflection you arrive at 'Cirencester', but not the strictly correct modern pronunciation, rendered phonetically as 'Cissister'.

Civitas capitals were self-governing communities, with a town council whose members and magistrates were responsible for keeping order within their territories, for collecting provincial and local taxes, and for jurisdiction of certain crimes committed within their boundaries. The town council was called the *ordo*, made up of decurions. The decurions of the colonies at Lincoln and York acquired the Roman epigraphic habit and recorded themselves on inscriptions, but unfortunately the members of the councils in the *civitas* capitals are as yet anonymous, either because they did not adopt the custom of recording personal information in this way, and did not set up tombstones, or because such inscriptions have eluded archaeologists. Corporate inscriptions on the other hand do survive. As mentioned above, the most important one is from Caerwent (*RIB* 311), because it sheds light on local government. The inscription is a dedication to Tiberius Claudius Paulinus, who had been legate of II Augusta, in which capacity he would have been based at Caerleon, close to Caerwent, and well known to the inhabitants. He had subsequently been appointed as governor of Gallia Narbonensis, and then eventually returned to Britain, as governor of the northern half of the island, not long after the Emperor Severus or possibly Caracalla had split Britain into two provinces. The dedication suggests that he was respected in Caerwent, and it was probably set up just before Paulinus returned to Britain. The most important part of the text reads *ex decreto ordinis respubl[ica] civi[atis] Silurum*, 'by decree of the council of the *civitas* of the Silures'. This not only shows the *ordo* making decisions and carrying them out, but reveals that the *civitas* was described as *respublica*, summing up its Roman-style corporate self-government. The term *respublica* did not simply refer to the capital itself, but comprised the whole territory of the tribe, including other satellite towns. The inscription from Kenchester declares the town to be within the *respublica Dobunnorum*, which was governed from Cirencester (Corinium Dobunnorum), and Brougham in Cumbria belonged to the *respublica Carvetiorum*, the Carvetii, whose capital was at Carlisle.

From the body of decurions, magistrates were elected, in pairs called *duoviri*, to carry out the administration of justice, organise tax collection, keep the streets clean and the buildings in good repair, just as in all towns and cities of the Empire, though on a more modest scale. They were also responsible for the territory of the *civitas* or tribe, and for maintaining order among the members of the tribe as well as the inhabitants of the smaller towns within their borders.

The men who formed the government of these *civitas* capitals as members of the *ordo* would require considerable wealth. They were expected to finance building projects and to embellish their towns out of their own pockets. A certain civic pride is detectable in the laconic inscriptions that have survived. The decurions, especially those who were elected as magistrates, would hope to achieve the respect of their communities, but unlike the magistrates of the *municipiae*, the chartered towns, they did not necessarily receive Roman citizenship after holding office, remaining in Roman eyes as *peregrini*, 'foreigners' or non-Romans. Since there is a dearth of personal inscriptions, it cannot be ascertained who these decurions were, or where they lived. It has been suggested that the *ordo* should normally comprise one hundred members, but in most of the *civitas* capitals there are not sufficient houses of the size and scale that would be expected of a council member, so most of the decurions perhaps lived in villas outside the town. Their wealth, like that of all other people of the Roman Empire, would derive mostly from landowning, or perhaps from trade, though nothing can be proved as to where or how the decurions earned a living. Being non-Romans, there was perhaps not the same degree of snobbishness among them about wealth derived from sources other than agriculture. Money from trade was perhaps more acceptable in Britain than it was in Rome, where senators were forbidden to engage in business, or in any kind of work, which was considered sordid. Senators circumvented the law and kept their hands clean by operating businesses at second hand via their middle-class agents, and grew respectably rich on the proceeds.

One of the distinguishing features of a *civitas* capital is considered to be the presence of administrative buildings, such as a Forum and a basilica where meetings could be held and legal processes carried out. This has been challenged, since it is possible to hold meetings without these appurtenances, which may explain why the development of these towns appears to have been rather slow. It was not until the Flavian period that most of these towns received a

Forum and basilica, as excavation after excavation has revealed. The main problem is that there is no secure dating evidence for the initial foundation of most of the *civitas* capitals. It has been noted above that the Romans would need to devolve some of the local administration onto the natives as quickly as possible, to relieve their own manpower of these tasks, but apart from Canterbury, where some buildings of Claudius's reign have come to light, and in the realm of Tiberius Claudius Togidubnus, it still seems that the main impetus for civic development occurred in the reigns of the Flavian Emperors.

This leads once again to the debate about Romanisation, whether it was deliberately fostered by the Roman authorities, or simply left to native initiative. Perhaps it was a combination of both. The native towns were frequently built on land that had just been vacated by the military, so apart from the south and south-east, it is perhaps not to be expected that there would be any development until campaigns started in the north of England and southern Scotland, in the early 70s AD, and various forts went out of use as the soldiers moved north. Cerialis, Frontinus, and Agricola would have a vested interest in fostering native self-government to release military and administrative staff and to ensure peace behind them while they campaigned. As mentioned above, it may have been Frontinus who established Caerwent, just after the final conquest of the Silures, but it took some time to flourish, and the town centre was not built up until the reign of Hadrian.

When the first *civitas* capitals were established, it has been suggested that the *iuridici* who were sent to Britain may have rendered assistance and given advice, but it is possible that other Roman officials were normally involved, not least to mark out territorial boundaries. In the undeveloped tribal areas of the Danube, a *praefectus civitatis* is attested in the early period of development, perhaps to oversee the foundation and administration of the first native self-governing communities. There is no hint of evidence for the same kind of officials in Britain, but it remains a possibility that officials did exist who have not found their way into the historical record. If there was never any official Flavian policy to develop *civitas* capitals in Britain, then the almost synchronised development of the towns requires explanation. Perhaps it was not always entirely due to local initiative, and rivalry and a sudden access of civic ambition will not entirely suffice. There was probably more proactive Romanisation than is currently fashionable among historians, and perhaps Tacitus's description of Agricola spending his winters encouraging the Britons should not be discounted.

The main development of *civitas* capitals occurred in the south of the island, except for Caistor-by-Norwich, which was not established until the second century. In the north, there were late additions to the list of such towns, such as the Brigantian capital at Aldborough, called Isurium Brigantum, not founded until after the Romans had overrun their territory. At Wroxeter (Viroconium Cornoviorum) the military forces were in occupation for some time, so that the development of the *civitas* had to wait until the reign of Hadrian, and at Carlisle the capital of the Carvetii is not attested until the middle of the third century.

Also available from Amberley Publishing

GREAT TALES
FROM BRITISH HISTORY

ON THE
EVE OF THE
TITANIC
DISASTER

W. B. BARTLETT